How to

Slay the ACT

2019-2020

Proven Strategies to Conquer

the College Entrance Exam

TINA WILES

DEDICATION

To Mike Wiles – Thank you for supporting me in every crazy idea I have. You are my everything!

To Jeremy, Josh, Luke, and Danny – Thank you for giving me a reason to laugh every day. Everything I do is to build a successful life for each of you!

To Mike and Janet Dobson (or as I call them, Mom and Dad) – Thank you for your never-ending love and support!

To all of my students – Thank you for teaching me how to be a great teacher!

ACKNOWLEDGMENTS

Thank you to Sydney Powers, my amazing editor.

Thank you to Tricia Dunn for being one of my biggest supporters!

CONTENTS

HOW TO USE THIS BOOK

Over my 11 years of tutoring the ACT, the best book I have found to prepare for the ACT is the book that the ACT publishes. At the time of this printing, the current book is *The Official ACT Prep Guide 2019-2020*. So many students buy this book, but few students know what to do with this book once they have it! *How to Slay the ACT* is a book to help you get the most out of *The Official ACT Prep Guide 2019-2020*.

Getting the most out of this book is as easy as counting to 5:

1. Take the first test in The Official ACT Prep Guide 2019-2020.

2. Score the test (see what you got right and wrong).

3. Look at the table on page 12 of this book and highlight the numbers of the questions that you got INCORRECT.

4. Review the section of *How to Slay the ACT* to understand the concept that you are struggling with AND learn how to apply test taking strategies to these types of problems.

5. Try the problems that are listed in *How to Slay the ACT* to ensure that you understand the concept that you were struggling with!

My hope is that this book will give students a game plan to best prepare for the ACT. Practicing, reviewing what you did wrong, and then using strategies and a review of the content on the exam to get the questions correct the next time!

Practice, practice, and more practice is what is going to make your score increase!

WHAT TO EXPECT ON THE TEST

How do they figure out my score?

Every test date has its own test. In other words, tests are never repeated. After a test is given, all the tests are sent to ACT where they are scored; the test is then "curved." Each section of the test is scored on a scale that goes from 1 (low) to 36 (high). If I told you that you got half of the questions wrong in a section, you would probably think that things didn't go so well. WRONG! The test is curved so that getting approximately half of the questions wrong in a section (or half of the questions right, depending on how you look at it) will give you a 20 in that section!

The national average on the ACT in 2018 was 20.8

Source: https://www.act.org/content/dam/act/unsecured/documents/cccr2018/Average-Scores-by-State.pdf

To give you an idea of what "good" scores are, here are some average scores to get into colleges across the country. Now before I give you some specific scores, I want to make sure that you are aware that getting a certain score on the ACT in no way guarantees admission to a college. There are many things considered during the acceptance process – GPA, test scores, extracurricular activities, etc.

 *Tutor Tina recommends making a list of schools that you are interested in and then go to their websites to look up the average scores for students that are admitted to each school.*

For Harvard or Yale, you will need a 33 or above. Most competitive state colleges are 25 and above, depending on where you live. State schools that aren't as competitive are usually 20 and above. If you are scoring below a 20, there is no reason to be upset. There are still many options and schools that you can go to!

How do they figure out the composite score? They take an average of the scores from each of the sections (English, Math, Reading, and Science), and the best news of all – they round up! If you scored an average of 20.5, congrats! That means that you scored a 21!

There are several trains of thought on how to increase your composite score. Obviously, increasing your scores in all the sections will increase your composite score, but doing extra work in the sections that you score *highest* and *lowest* in can also *increase* your score. Let's look at an example:

Let's say you scored the following:

Composite: 22

English: 24
Math: 22
Reading: 22
Science: 20

After you learn the tips and tricks for English and Science, you get the following scores:

Composite: 24

English: 26
Math: 22
Reading: 22
Science: 24

The lowest (Science) and highest (English) both increased, but Math and Reading stayed the same. Focusing on this student's strength and weakness resulted in a two-point increase!

OVERALL STRUCTURE OF THE TEST

English Section

Timing

- 75 questions in 45 minutes

- 5 passages, each with about 15 questions

- If you are going to have enough time to complete the entire English test, you should be spending 9 minutes per passage. You don't have to spend 9 minutes on each passage, but if you want to finish the English section without having to guess on questions, you cannot spend **more** than 9 minutes per passage. I will talk in the English section of this book about what to do IF you have extra time on this section.

Types of questions

Conventions (38-42 questions)
Production of Writing (22-24 questions)
Knowledge of Language (10-14 questions)

Math Section

Timing

- 60 questions in 60 minutes

- You have 1 minute per question if you want to finish all 60 questions, but if Math isn't your strong suit, I will talk about how to get your highest score in the Math section. You will be surprised that you can score higher by focusing on the easier problems!

Types of questions

The general trend is from easy to hard as you progress through the Math Section.

Higher Math (34-36 questions) **Higher Math does NOT mean Harder Math**

Number and Quantity (4-6 questions)

Algebra (7-9 questions)

Functions (7-9 questions)

Geometry (7-9 questions)

Statistics and Probability (5-7 questions)

Integrating Essential Skills (24-26 questions)

Reading Section

Timing

- 40 questions in 35 minutes

- 4 passages, each with 10 questions

- You have approximately 8 minutes and 30 seconds per passage if you plan to read all 4 passages. This is difficult to do for most students, and we will discuss in the Reading section how to plan to get your highest score.

Types of passages

Literary Narrative or Prose Fiction

Social Studies

Humanities

Natural Science

Types of questions

Key Ideas and Details (22-24 questions)

Craft and Structure (10-12 questions)

Integration of Knowledge and Ideas (5-7 questions)

Science Section

Timing

- 40 questions in 35 minutes

- 6-7 passages

- Approximately 5-7 minutes per passage

Types of passages

Data Representation (12-16 questions)

Research Summaries (18-22 questions)

Conflicting Viewpoints (6-8 questions)

Types of questions

Interpretation of Data (18-22 questions)

Scientific Investigation (8-12 questions)

Understanding the relationship between the provided information and the conclusions (1-4 questions)

Writing Section (optional)

Timing

- 1 prompt in 40 minutes

Persuasive Essay

Describes an issue and provides 3 different perspectives

"Evaluate and analyze" the perspectives

"State and develop" your own perspective

"Explain the relationship" between your perspective and those given

START HERE!!

Coming up with a plan before you start preparing is very important. Unfortunately, the ACT is NOT a test that you can cram for the night before. If you do, there is a good chance that you will be disappointed with your score. To get your highest score possible, think about attacking the test like an athlete getting ready for the game of your life!

How does this book work?

The whole idea behind this book is to give you STRUCTURE while preparing for the test. I have helped students prepare and kick butt on the ACT for over 13 years. I love this test (I'm not sure why), and I want to use my passion for this test to help *you*!

The *Official ACT Prep Guide 2019-2020* is *the* book for helping you prepare for the test, but I have found many students aren't sure what to do with the book once they have it. This book is intended to go along with the *Official ACT Prep Guide 2019-2020* (referred to for the rest of this book as the Red Book).

Step 1. Figure out which plan is right for you.

Step 2. Take the first practice test to see where your strengths and weaknesses lie.

Step 3. Attack your practice per the plan that is right for you (use the second, third, and fourth tests in the Red Book for practice and timing exercises).

Step 4. Take the fifth practice test in the Official Prep Guide to see how things progressed.

Step 5. Kick some ACT….

Step 1. Which plan is right for you?

Super prepared student

If you are the type of student that does all the practice problems that a teacher assigns even though you know the teacher is never going to collect them, then this is the plan for you.

6 weeks before the test:

- Take the first test in the Red Book to get a baseline score. Review the Explanatory Answers for the questions that you got wrong.
- Use the following table (page 12) to figure out the sections of this book that you need to review.
- Count the total number of sections that you need to review, and then divide the total by 4 to know how many sections you need to review a week for weeks 5, 4, 3, and 2.
- Put a 5 next to the sections for Week 5, a 4 next to the sections for Week 4, etc.

5 weeks before the test:

- Review week 5 sections of the *How to Slay* book and do the corresponding problems in the Red Book.
- Check answers and explanations of the problems that you are doing in the Red Book.

4 weeks before the test:

- Review week 4 sections of the *How to Slay* book and do the corresponding problems in the Red Book.
- Check answers and explanations of the problems that you are doing in the Red Book.

3 weeks before the test:

- Review week 3 sections of the *How to Slay* book and do the corresponding problems in the Red Book.
- Check answers and explanations of the problems that you are doing in the Red Book.

2 weeks before the test:

- Review week 2 sections of the *How to Slay* book and do the corresponding problems in the Red Book.
- Check answers and explanations of the problems that you are doing in the Red Book.

1 week before the test:

- Take the fifth practice test in the Red Book. Review the Explanatory Answers for the questions that you got wrong.
- Review the sections of *How to Slay* for the questions that you got wrong.

Motivated student

If you are the type of student that does the work that needs to be done but are super busy and can't commit to spending hours a week preparing for the test, then this is the plan for you.

4 weeks before test:

- Take the first test in the Red Book to get a baseline score. Review the Explanatory Answers for the questions that you got wrong.
- Use the following table (page 12) to figure out the sections of this book that you need to review.

3 weeks before the test:

- Review the sections of the *How to Slay* book for the section that you scored *worst* in and do the corresponding problems in the Red Book.
- Check answers and explanations of the problems that you are doing in the Red Book.

2 weeks before the test:

- Review the sections of the *How to Slay* book for the section that you scored *best* in and do the corresponding problems in the Red Book.
- Check answers and explanations of the problems that you are doing in the Red Book.
- Review anything else you would like to refresh in the *How to Slay* book.

1 week before the test:

- Take the fifth practice test in the Red Book.
- Review the Explanatory Answers for the questions that you got wrong.
- Review the sections of *How to Slay* for the questions that you got wrong.

The ACT is in 7 days – HELP!!!

If you are the student that the test just kind of snuck up on, then here is a 7-day boot camp to help you prepare.

Day 1: Take the first test in the Red Book to get a baseline score.

Review the Explanatory Answers for the questions that you got wrong.

Day 2: Use the following table (page 12) to figure out what sections of this book that you need to review.

Day 3: Review the section of the test that you scored HIGHEST in the *How to Slay* book and do the corresponding problems in the Red Book. Check answers and explanations of the problems that you are doing in the Red Book.

Day 4: Review the section of the test that you scored LOWEST in the *How to Slay* book and do the corresponding problems in the Red Book. Check answers and explanations of the problems that you are doing in the Red Book

Day 5: Take the fifth practice test in the Red Book. Review the Explanatory Answers for the questions that you got wrong. Review the sections of *How to Slay* for the questions that you got wrong.

Day 6: Review anything you are struggling with in the *How to Slay* book.

Day 7: Take that test and do AMAZING!

Working through practice problems on your own can be very tough. It is hard to stay on a schedule for practicing when no one is bugging you about due dates. So, you need to figure out before you start working through this book what you are going to use for motivation. Do you have a dream school that you need a certain score to get into? Do you need to hit a score to get a scholarship? Do you have a sibling or a friend that you want to score higher than?

Answer the following questions in the front cover of your Red Book:

What is your plan to reach that goal score?

What is your inspiration that will keep you motivated to practice?

Step 2. Take the First Test in the Red Book

What makes standardized testing so difficult?

- Staying **focused** for so long

- **Time** limits for each section

- Getting stuck on **hard** problems

- Making silly **mistakes** on easy problems

The fastest way to improve is to figure out where you are weak and do some work on it! The best way to figure out where your weakness lies is to take a full practice test. It is best if you can do this all in one sitting. I know it's hard to carve out 3.5 hours in your busy schedule, but one of the toughest things about standardized tests is that you need to think so hard for so long. If you can practice building up your "testing endurance," it will only help you once test day rolls around. If you can't fit the entire test in at once, do your best to still stick to the timing. What I mean by that, is when you sit down to take the practice test, give yourself 45 minutes to take the English test and so on.

Timing is something that is difficult on a test. Some of you might move too fast and make silly errors, while others might not leave enough time to finish certain sections (the reading section is the most common section to run out of time during).

After you take the first test in the Red Book, you need to spend some time scoring it. The answers to the questions are found immediately following the test, and you need to make sure that you are using the scaled scores for the appropriate test because the scaled scores on each test vary!

So now it is time to make the magic happen. Here is the secret to using this book! Either mark in the table on page 12 OR use a separate sheet to figure out which questions you got wrong. Use the table to figure out which sections of this book you need to read first, and then do the practice problems following the topic that you need to work on.

ENGLISH SECTION		
Questions you got wrong	**Read this section of** *How to Slay the ACT*	**Page Number**
2, 41, 71	Adverb/Adjective Confusion	31
9, 11, 14, 17, 26, 34, 38, 46, 52, 58, 69, 72, 73	Clear and Concise Writing	39
4, 15, 23, 30, 32, 37, 40, 44, 54, 57, 59, 65, 68, 75	Content	36
63	Idioms	41
22	Modifiers	30
13, 29, 45, 55, 60, 62, 70, 74	Organizing Ideas	37
25	Parallelism	26
48	Possessive/Plural	35
42, 48	Pronouns	27
1, 3, 5, 18, 20, 21, 28, 35, 36, 39, 47, 53, 61, 64	Punctuation	32
8, 43, 49, 51	Sentence Structure	22
67	Shifts in Construction	25
24	Subject/Verb Agreement	27
6, 26, 52	Transitions	38
7, 12, 16, 19, 31, 33, 56, 66	Verb Tense	28

10, 27, 50, 63	Word Choice	41
MATH SECTION		
Questions you got wrong	**Read this section of** *How to Slay the ACT*	**Page Number**
26	Absolute Value Equations	81
16	Angles and Lines	96
11, 21, 32	Area	103
3, 42	Basic Operations	50
15	Binomials & Quadratics	77
27, 35, 55, 58	Circles	100co
1, 47	Combining Terms	60
42	Complex Numbers	67
27	Conics	114
24	Data Collection	117
34, 36, 37	Distance	93
1	Distribution	73
	Domain and Range	87
60	Expected Value	117
53, 56	Exponents	71
15, 47	Factoring	75
23, 25	Factors and Multiples	52
5, 10, 18	Functions	86

18, 19, 20	Comparisons Between Passages	139
21, 28, 34	Determine Main Ideas	130
5, 7, 22, 26	Draw Generalizations	138
1, 4, 8, 9, 10, 11, 14, 23, 24, 25, 27, 29, 30, 35, 36, 37, 38, 39, 40	Locate Significant Details	128
12, 13, 15, 32	Rhetorical Devices and Literary Techniques	135
16	Sequence of Events	132
6, 17, 33	Vocabulary in Context	133

SCIENCE SECTION

Questions you got wrong	Read this section of *How to Slay the ACT*	Page Number
18	Analysis	158
16, 17, 19, 20	Compare Alternate Viewpoints	156
10, 24, 26, 28, 32	Design of Experiments	157
1, 2, 3, 4, 5, 6, 35, 36, 37, 38, 39, 40	Graph Reading	149
7, 8, 9, 11, 12, 13, 21, 22, 23, 25, 29, 30, 31, 33, 34	Interpretation of Experimental Results	154
5	Interpretation of Information Presented	151

14, 15, 27	Understanding	159

Step 3. Practice

Practice per the plan that works best for your situation. Always make sure to keep the overall timing for each of the sections in mind. In each section of *How to Slay*, I have put practice problems for both the second and third practice tests in the Red Book. It would be great if you only need to use the second, third, and fourth tests for practice.

Step 4. Take the third practice test in the Red Book to see how things progressed!

If you used the third practice test in the Red Book for practice, go to My2tor.com to get access to a free practice test that you can take!

Step 5. Kick some ACT….

ENGLISH

PETITE

SHORT AND SIMPLE WILL HELP
YOU GET A HIGHER SCORE!

Strategy

What does petite mean to you?

When I hear petite, I think short, and that is what you want to keep in mind during the English section of the test – short and simple! The English section is testing that you are choosing the shortest, grammatically correct answer. In fact, if you just go through a test and look at the correct answers, it is crazy how often the shortest, simplest answer is the correct answer choice!

Now should you go through and choose the shortest answer for every problem on the English test? Probably not because you will score a 14, but this is a great first step to our strategy!

Keep an eye out for the following two illustrations in this chapter. The elephants are placed to show you where the Petite concept is used. The Tutor Tina will give tips throughout the book!

> *Game Plan for English*
>
> *1. Read the passage until you get to a question.*
>
> *2. Plug in the petite, simplest answer.*
>
> *3. Reread the entire sentence.*

So let's go into the game plan in a little more detail.

1. **Read the passage until you get to a question.**

   A. It is extremely important to read the *entire* passage. Now I know that you may be thinking that you can save time by not reading, but in the long run, you might be sacrificing some easy questions on the test. Without reading, the questions that are about the story are almost impossible!

   B. 40-60% of the questions are rhetorical (about the story), so it is well worth the time to read everything! These questions will be very difficult to get correct if you don't understand what the story is trying to tell you.

2. **Plug in the petite (simplest) answer.**

   I know that it sounds super easy, but start with the shortest answer choice!

   Example 1:

   The teacher determined that the student's score improved after using the <u>process, which was discovered by trial and error.</u>

   A.   NO CHANGE
   B.   process, which is exactly what the teacher was hoping for.
   C.   process, a process he practiced for weeks.
   D.   process.

   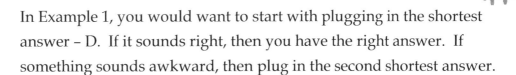

   In Example 1, you would want to start with plugging in the shortest answer – D. If it sounds right, then you have the right answer. If something sounds awkward, then plug in the second shortest answer.

Example 2:

The <u>word itself</u> comes from the French word for cheese, *frommage*.

    F.   NO CHANGE
    G.   word, itself,
    H.   word, itself
    J.   word itself,

For Example 2, you want to start with the answer that has the fewest punctuation marks, which happens to be choice F. In this case, F is the correct answer. G is wrong because if the word "itself" is surrounded by commas, you would be able to remove the word from sentence. If you remove "itself," then you don't know which word comes from *frommage*. The other two answers are incorrect because they break up the sentence in an awkward place (which you will know after you use Step 3).

3. Reread the entire sentence.

There are a lot of times that the wrong answer sounds like it is correct when you are only reading part of the sentence, but when you read the answer into the entire sentence, it will sound awkward.

 Tutor Tina says that the number one reason for getting a question wrong on the English section is that the answer sounds correct when you are looking at what is underlined, but the answer is incorrect when you read it in the full sentence.

Example 3:

The sky <u>was</u> cloudy: this sounds correct, but when I look at the entire sentence, it is obvious that it is wrong for question.

My sister said that today the weather is supposed to be sunny, but the sky <u>was</u> cloudy.

    A.   NO CHANGE
    B.   will be
    C.   is
    D.   isn't

In Example 3, if you are only looking right around the underlined word, any of the answer choices would work, and it would be very easy to get this question wrong. The key is reading the entire sentence because due to the word "today", the sentence is present tense. This means that C is the correct answer.

Now that you know the game plan for approaching the questions on the English test, let's take a look at the types of questions you are going to see on the test.

English Timing/Scoring

It is important to keep in mind the timing for the English section. You have 5 passages in 45 minutes, which breaks down to about 9 minutes per passage. Each passage has 15 questions. Some important tips to keep in mind:

- Keep moving forward through the test. If you have to read a question more than twice, try skipping it and then coming back to it.
- If you struggle with timing:
  - There is no doubt in my mind that if you had as much time as you needed, you would do amazing. The tricky part is telling yourself it is OK to guess on the hard problems!
  - If you keep getting stuck between two answer choices, look for what has to be wrong with one of them instead of what *sounds* right to you.
- If you have extra time:
  - If you have circled your answer choices in the test book, you can go back and reread the "story" with your answer choices plugged in.
- Getting about **4** questions wrong per passage will put you around a **26!**

Conventions of Standard English (38-52 questions)

Sentence Structure

The most common question on the English section has to deal with sentence structure.

An independent clause is a group of words that stands by itself as a complete sentence. It has a subject, a verb, and a complete thought.

She walks.

She walks to the store.

She walks to the store to get the ingredients to make dinner.

> *For a complete sentence you need:*
>
> 1. *Subject.*
>
> 2. *Verb.*
>
> 3. *Complete thought.*

A dependent clause is a group of words that has a subject and verb, but it does NOT form a complete thought. To be a complete sentence, a dependent clause needs to be combined with an independent clause.

After going to the store,

When we got to class,

Both examples are incomplete thoughts; they leave you wondering what is going on.

Which of these two examples is a complete sentence?

A. After going away to college, people from all over the country.
B. After going away to college, I met people from all over the country.

When I look at choice A, the beginning of the sentence is a dependent clause, so I don't even need to look at that. So, I look at what is after the comma, "people from all over the country." This isn't a complete thought because it is missing a verb!

Choice B starts with a dependent clause as well, so I'll look after the comma: "I met people from all over the country." This is a complete thought – it has a subject and a verb. Choice B is the complete sentence.

Now that you know the difference between independent and dependent clauses, let's talk about run on sentences and sentence fragments.

Run-on sentences are sentences that keep going and have way too many ideas in one sentence which makes them hard to read because you don't know where one idea ends and the next one begins. (Do you like my example of a run-on sentence?)

Jeremy is very funny he loves to tell jokes.

What are three ways that we can correct this sentence?

a. **Add a period:** We can simply make this two sentences. Jeremy is very funny. He loves to tell jokes.

b. **Use a semicolon:** This might not be something that you use commonly, but it appears **ALL THE TIME** on the test. A semicolon can be used in place of a period. Jeremy is very funny; he loves to tell jokes.

c. **Comma and a conjunction:** You can add two independent clauses together with a comma and a conjunction. Have you ever heard of FANBOYS (stands for: **F**or **A**nd **N**or **B**ut **O**r **Y**et **S**o)? FANBOYS are common conjunctions that can be used with a comma. If you have a comma and a conjunction, you need to have a complete sentence on either side of it! Jeremy is very funny, and he loves to tell jokes.

Tina says to replace every semicolon you see on the ACT with a period! It is the easiest way to see if you can use a semicolon. You need a complete sentence on either side.

23

*Just to help you with your papers for English class, I should also note that you can only use a semicolon to combine two sentences when the sentences have something to do with each other.

The other extreme in sentence construction is a **sentence fragment**; a sentence fragment is a type of dependent clause. It is not a complete sentence.

Joshua loves to hunt for crystals. And pretend that he is Indiana Jones.

Which of these two "sentences" is a sentence fragment? I sure hope that you said the second "sentence." It is not a complete thought. In English terms, it is missing the subject. Remember that a complete sentence needs a subject, verb, and a complete thought. Can you fix the sentence above about Joshua by replacing the period with a comma? NO!!! If you use a comma and a conjunction, you would be able to replace them with a period and have two complete sentences. "Pretend that he is Indiana Jones" is not a complete sentence because it doesn't have a subject.

Example 4:

The music is mainly <u>rock – the bands generally</u> consist of guitar, bass guitar, and drums.
Which of the following alternatives to the underlined portion would **NOT** be acceptable?
    F. rock; in general, the bands
    G. rock, the bands generally
    H. rock. The bands generally
    J. rock; the band generally

Well, from what I said already, hopefully you remember that a semicolon and a period are the same thing. With that said, choices H and J are EXACTLY the same!!! So you can eliminate both of them! The correct answer for Example 4 is G because in order to combine two complete sentences, you need to use a comma and a conjunction. If you think that I put down the incorrect answer to this question, you probably missed the word NOT in the question itself.

Practice Problems:

Red Book Test 2	Red Book Test 3	Red Book Test 4	Red Book Test 5
23, 26, 36, 49, 56	4, 16, 21, 29, 32, 59, 65	6, 15, 56, 66	58

Shifts in Construction

There are several types of shifts in sentence construction that are on the test. A shift is when things change midsentence or mid-paragraph.

Shifts in verb tense:

A sentence has to have the same verb tense throughout the sentence. If a sentence shifts between past, present, and future verb tenses, it was the wrong answer. Oops, did you see what I did in the sentence? Did it sound funny when you read it? It should have! The first part of the sentence ("If a sentence shifts between….") is in the present tense: shifts. The second part of the sentence ("it was the wrong…") shifts to the past tense: was.

Shifts in person or number:

A doctor needs years of training before they get a medical license. Why does this sentence sound wrong? This is an example of a shift in number of people. The beginning part of the sentence refers to "a doctor," but the second part of the sentence has "they." In order to get a question like this correct on the test, you MUST maintain the same number of people throughout the entire sentence. The sentence should read, "A doctor needs years of training before he/she gets a medical license."

Shift in voice:

There are three types of voice that are used when writing:

- First person (I, we)
- Second person (you)
- Third person (he/she, they)

This type of shift does not occur often on the test, but I hope that it will stick out like a sore thumb when it does. An entire essay might say "when you do this" or "when you do that," and then it might get to a question that tries to change it to "I". If the essay has been written in second person, it needs to maintain the second person point of view throughout the entire essay.

Practice Problems:

Red Book Test 2	Red Book Test 3	Red Book Test 4	Red Book Test 5
25	None	34	None

Parallelism

Parallelism sure sounds like it should be in the Math section and not the grammar section! Don't worry – we will talk about it in math too! Parallelism in English is the principle that grammatical elements with the same function need to have the same form.

Example 5:

Luke's trip included going to the museum, <u>visit</u> with a friend, and swimming.

    A. NO CHANGE
    B. visited
    C. will visit
    D. visiting

In this sentence, the verbs all need to have the same form because they have the same function. The other verbs are "going" and "swimming," so the underlined word (visit) needs to end in -ing as well. D is the correct answer.

Practice Problems:

Red Book Test 2	Red Book Test 3	Red Book Test 4	Red Book Test 5
5	9, 12, 56, 58, 61	None	43

Subject and Verb Agreement

It might seem silly talking about this for a college admission test ; you have been working on subject verb agreement since you started writing sentences in elementary school, but some of the questions can be deceiving. When you have to pick a verb, make sure you know what the subject is before you choose your answer.

a.   The paint on the walls <u>is/are</u> blue.

b.   On the volleyball court, Brandon and Andrew <u>is/are</u> great teammates.

For choice a, the answer is "is" because even though "walls" is next to the verb, the subject of the sentence is "paint". For b, the answer is "are" because the subject is plural (both Brandon and Andrew.)

Pronouns

Now I know that you have been working with nouns and pronouns for what feels like FOREVER, but I am always surprised when students aren't sure what pronouns are. You know that nouns are person, places, or things (and some teachers now add ideas to the list). Pronouns are words that can replace a noun. Example of pronouns are: she, he, we, they, I, you, us, and it. The single most important thing that you need to remember when working on pronoun questions is that you NEED to know what the pronoun is replacing in order to choose the correct answer. It sounds easy, but a pronoun needs to match what it refers to in both quantity and gender.

Andrew went to the Bulls game and brought his / their friends.

Seems straightforward enough. The pronoun is replacing the word "Andrew," so it needs to be "his" friends. The questions aren't always this straightforward on the test though!

Somethings to keep in mind regarding pronouns:
Who, whom and whose refer to people.
Which, what, and that refer to things.

And now it is time for one of the most common questions I am asked regarding the entire English test. (Insert drumroll here!) ***What is the difference between who and whom?*** Here are two answers to that question. The first one you will remember for the test, and the second one is the actual grammatical reason behind the answer.

1. How often do you use the word *whom* when you are speaking? Pretty much never, right? That is how often you are going to choose *whom* as an answer on the test. It is almost NEVER correct.

2. *Who* is used when you are using the pronoun to replace the subject, and *whom* is used when you are using the pronoun as a direct or indirect object. In other words, you can use *whom* if you have a preposition in front of it (to, from, at, etc.) The perfect example of this is "to whom it may concern." Another way to remember it is that who is like he and whom is like him (whom and him both end with the letter "m".)

 *Take some advice from Tina:* <u>Whom</u> *is the correct answer on the test pretty much as often as you use it when you are talking- which is pretty much* <u>**NEVER**</u>*!!!*

Practice Problems:

Red Book Test 2	Red Book Test 3	Red Book Test 4	Red Book Test 5
25, 32, 41, 46, 54	51, 69	7, 33, 58	6, 51, 71

Verb Tense

What is wrong with the following sentence?: Last week, Samah goes on a cruise. "Last week" is a clue to the verb tense that needs to be used in the sentence. The sentence needs to be written in past tense, but the verb "goes" is present tense. If you are having a difficult time with the tense in one sentence, look at the sentences around it to help give you a clue!

Now to throw a little more confusion into the verb tense topic: when "had," "has," or "have" is in the verb, it is used to show timing. It gives you the sense of a timeline. For example, Emily had gone on a cruise and realized that she forgot her bathing suit! This shows that Emily going on the cruise occurred BEFORE she realized she forgot her bathing suit.

Let's conjugate the verb *dance* just to have some fun!

Present tense: action is taking place now. (dance)
Present perfect tense: action is occurring over time. (has danced)
Past tense: action happened in the past. (danced)
Past perfect tense: action took place before another specified action. (had danced)
Future tense: action will happen in the future. (will dance)
Future perfect tense: action will continue to happen until a certain point. (will have danced)

Example 6:

As the baby slept through the night, the parents <u>were also sleeping</u> and starting to feel like human beings again.

    F.   NO CHANGE
    G.   are also sleeping
    H.   have also sleeping
    J.   will also sleeping

In Example 6, the clause at the beginning of the sentence gives you the only hint that you need in order to figure out what the tense of the underlined verb needs to be. Since the baby *slept* is in past tense, the answer choice needs to be in the past tense as well! The only answer that works is A.

Example 7:

In the 1980's, the dancers <u>have borrowed</u> most of their moves from Michael Jackson.

    A. NO CHANGE
    B. have been borrowing
    C. were borrowed
    D. borrowed

The year is a HUGE hint in Example 7. Because it is in the past, the verb needs to be past tense. This is also an example of where the Petite answer applies!!! Hopefully you went with answer D because that is the right answer!

Practice Problems:

Red Book Test 2	Red Book Test 3	Red Book Test 4	Red Book Test 5
3, 5, 6, 11, 24, 35, 42, 48, 53, 69, 71	8, 12, 24, 31, 42, 46, 52, 64	28, 38, 50, 67	18, 26, 33, 42, 46, 53, 64, 66, 70

Modifiers

What is a modifier? It is a noun or adjective that adds description to a sentence.

Luke found the gold man's watch.

Hmmm, something is wrong with this sentence. The modifier is in the wrong place in the sentence; a modifier needs to be next to what it is modifying ("gold watch" not "gold man's").

Example 8: The employee sold the hat to the woman <u>with the blue pattern</u>.

Which of the following would be an acceptable placement for the underlined portion:

    A. where it is now.
    B. at the beginning of the sentence (revising the capitalization accordingly).
    C. after the word <u>hat</u>.
    D. after the word employee.

One way to solve this would be to plug in each answer choice to see what "sounds" best to you. This will work but might take a little time. The other way to approach this problem would be to ask yourself, "what has the blue pattern?" Remember, the modifier needs to be next to what it is modifying (or describing). The hat has a blue pattern, so the phrase "with the blue pattern" needs to be next to the word "hat." C is the correct answer.

Practice Problems:

Red Book Test 2	Red Book Test 3	Red Book Test 4	Red Book Test 5
21, 68	14, 18, 21, 27, 38	23	65

Adverb/Adjective Confusion

Before we can talk about how adverb and adjectives are confused, let's define what they are:

Adverbs are words that are used to change or qualify the meaning of a verb, another adverb, pronoun, or clause. An adverb usually answers one of the following questions: when, where, how, to what extent, or in what way?

Adverbs:

Janet was walking <u>rapidly</u>.

The boys love playing Xbox <u>together.</u>

Please come inside <u>now</u>.

Adjectives are words that describe nouns or pronouns, and they are usually placed before the noun or the pronoun that they describe.

Adjectives:

They live in a <u>beautiful</u> house   .

The glass is <u>breakable</u>. (breakable is an adjective because it describes glass)

I met a <u>homeless</u> person in Chicago.

No practice problems in the Red Book.

As you can see, these types of questions do not appear often on the test!

Punctuation

When do you use a comma?

A comma and conjunction (FANBOYS – For And Nor But Or Yet So) separates two complete sentences.

Kyle gets to have his car in the auto show, so he is going to get new rims.

Remember that a period = a semicolon (;) = a comma and a conjunction.

If you have a comma near the beginning of a sentence, you can take out what is before the comma and the rest of the sentence will still make sense.

After practicing for weeks, Maddie did amazing at her orchestra performance!

Say, did you pass your history test?

Surrounding words by commas means that you can take out what is between the commas and everything else in the sentence will still make sense.

The free concert, in my opinion, is the place to be today.

The ACT, a test for college entrance, is much easier after practice.

If you have a comma near the beginning of a sentence, you can take out what is before the comma and the rest of the sentence will still make sense.

One of the best movies to watch on the 4th of July is *Independence Day*, in my opinion.

To separate adjectives. If you can switch the adjectives, you need to use a comma!

Julia throws a fast, low pitch when we play softball. We can switch this around to say "Julia throws a low, fast pitch."

To separate items in a list or series.

Lauren packed her suitcase, put on her jacket, and left for school.

Use commas in dates, addresses, place names, numbers, and quotations. (This doesn't appear on the ACT, but it is good to know for your own knowledge.)

Tina says the best website to use for comma practice is Purdue OWL https://owl.english.purdue.edu/owl/resource/692/01/

To check to see if you need to add or delete a comma:

-Try reading the sentence with extremely long pauses where there are commas. It might make it easier to "hear" if the commas are in the correct places.

-Check to see if the sentence still makes sense when you remove what is surrounded by commas.

When do you use a colon?

- Before a list.

Please bring the following books home: Algebra, Chemistry, and Spanish.

- After an independent clause that is followed by information that directly modifies or adds to the clause.

Sophie encountered a problem that she had not anticipated: a pop quiz.

The example above is the most common way of using a colon on the ACT.

When do you use a semicolon?

The easiest thing to remember is that you can ALWAYS replace a semicolon with a period.

To join closely related independent clauses when a coordinate conjunction is not used.

Noopur starts a new job today; she is very excited.

With conjunctive adverbs to join independent clauses.

Henry is great at baseball; he is one of the most valuable players on the team.

To separate items arranged in series that contain commas.

My first meal at college consisted of cold, dry toast; runny, undercooked eggs; and very strong coffee.

To separate coordinate clauses when they are joined by transitional words or phrases.

Mike often misplaces his keys; perhaps he should get a something that beeps when he loses them.

When do you use a dash?

Dashes are another way to sperate information that is NOT necessary to the sentence. The information is often defining or adding something to the sentence. Just like the commas, when words are surrounded by dashes, you can take the words out and the rest of the sentence makes sense.

Luke watches his favorite movies – Star Wars Return of the Jedi and Avenger's End Game – when he is not feeling well.

Today is the day I have to do one of my least favorite things – go to the dentist.

Practice Problems:

Red Book Test 2	Red Book Test 3	Red Book Test 4	Red Book Test 5
16, 19, 23, 31, 38, 40, 45, 47, 50, 63	1, 4, 10, 16, 20, 28, 32, 34, 41, 48, 50, 53, 59, 67	3, 8, 11, 16, 19, 27, 30, 41, 45, 46, 47, 49, 51, 53, 65, 72	2, 4, 19, 22, 25, 34, 39, 41, 48, 55, 56, 68

Possessive/Plural

When you are trying to decide if a word is possessive (meaning it needs an apostrophe), you need to ask yourself two questions.

1. Does the second word belong to the first word? If yes, then you need an apostrophe. If no, then you don't!
2. If you do need an apostrophe, look at the FIRST word to determine if it is singular or plural. If it is singular, then you will use 's. If the FIRST word is plural, then you will use s'.

- Add an apostrophe and an *s* to form the possessive of singular nouns, plural nouns, or indefinite pronouns that do not end in *s*.

    My friend's house is at the end of the street.

- Add an apostrophe to form the possessive of plural nouns ending in s.

    The horses' stalls were filled with straw.

- Add an apostrophe to the last noun to indicate joint possession.

    Mom and Dad's anniversary is in January.

- Add an apostrophe to all nouns to indicate individual possession.

    Lisa's and Grant's finals are over!

- Add an apostrophe to indicate contractions.

    If you're going to the movies, you better leave soon.

One that you will FOR SURE see on the test is:
"it's" means it is   "its" is used for possession   "its'" is NEVER the answer

Practice Problems:

Red Book Test 2	Red Book Test 3	Red Book Test 4	Red Book Test 5
1, 33, 58	19, 23, 33, 48	48, 72	3, 62

Production of Writing (21-24 questions)

Now it is time to finally talk about some of the non-usage and mechanics questions on the test! Strategy questions are one of the reasons that it is important to read what is in the essay between the questions. These are SO difficult if you aren't paying attention to what you are reading as you go through the passage!

Content

The majority of the questions regarding content on the English section are ACTUAL questions that you need to read (shocking!) instead of just having to plug in the answer choices. Because of that, a lot of these questions don't necessarily follow the PETITE rule that we talked about earlier. These questions don't always use the shortest answer because they are more about what the answer choices are about. The better strategy for content questions is to pick KEYWORDS out of the question. There are a lot of words on the English test, but by focusing on the KEYWORDS, it will be easier to get to the answer!

 *Strategy questions are easier to answer if you pick **KEYWORDS** out of the question!*

A couple questions on the test will be "**Suppose the writer**" questions. These questions will be at the end of a passage, and they will give you an "assignment" and then ask if this essay would fulfill the assignment. BEFORE you read the question, go back and reread the TITLE of the essay; after all, the title of the essay will tell you what the author's main idea is! NOW read the question and answer YES or NO only! NOW look only at the reasoning for the two answers that are now possibilities. The reasoning that is correct will always have to do with what an essay <u>does</u> talk about instead of what it <u>doesn't</u> talk about. This will make it easier to answer the question!

When asked a question about **<u>adding or deleting material</u>**, ask yourself if the information has material that helps the passage. If it does, you need it. If it doesn't, leave it out! ☺ Sounds easy, doesn't it? These can be harder though when you are short on time!

Example 9:

Which choices would most clearly communicate the fans' positive attitude toward this win?

<u>With great enthusiasm,</u> the Michigan Wolverines celebrated the National Championship. (Can you tell where I went to college? LOL)

A. NO CHANGE
B. Disappointingly,
C. Sadly,
D. In conclusion,

We need to look at what the keywords are in the questions. I would say that they are **positive attitude**, so we need to find the one and only answer choice that reflects those keywords. The correct answer is A.

Practice Problems:

Red Book Test 2	Red Book Test 3	Red Book Test 4	Red Book Test 4
2, 4, 8, 9, 15, 20, 27, 39, 55, 60, 62, 64, 74, 75	2, 5, 15, 25, 30, 36, 37, 44, 45, 54, 55, 60, 62, 63, 68, 70, 75	2, 4, 5, 14, 22, 25, 32, 39, 44, 59, 62, 63, 68	1, 13, 24, 30, 44, 47, 57, 60, 61, 63, 67, 72, 74

Organizing Ideas

Organization in an essay is developing logical sequences. You can tell when you are going to have an organizing ideas question because there are either numbers BEFORE each paragraph or numbers at the BEGINNING of each sentence. I have seen students get these questions wrong simply because they didn't realize that the paragraph or sentence numbers were in front of the paragraph/question to which the number is referring. With these types of questions, things usually sound awkward if they are out of place. In other words, you will be reading a passage and then all of a sudden you won't know what it is talking about. That means that a sentence or paragraph is out of order. DON'T BE AFRAID to choose NO CHANGE on these questions! If things didn't sound weird, then don't try to move things around!

Practice Problems:

Red Book Test 2	Red Book Test 3	Red Book Test 4	Red Book Test 5
14, 22, 51, 59	11, 35	13, 18, 71, 75	15, 23, 38, 45, 54, 59, 75

Transitions

To make sure that transitions are correct, look at the ideas before and after the transition and how they compare to each other. If you still aren't sure, you can eliminate words that have the same meaning.

There are several types of transitions (along with examples!):

Adding: as well as, moreover, additionally, furthermore

Sequencing: finally, meanwhile

Illustrating: for example, such as, for instance

Cause and effect: so, therefore, consequently

Comparing: similarly, as with, likewise

Qualifying: however, although, except, as long as

Contrasting: whereas, instead of, otherwise, on the other hand

Emphasizing: above all, especially, indeed

Many times on the test, there will be an option to NOT use a transition. This is usually the correct answer when it is an option. Are you surprised? It is the Petite answer!

Practice Problems:

Red Book Test 2	Red Book Test 3	Red Book Test 4	Red Book Test 5
18, 29, 52, 67	13, 17, 22, 66, 73	31, 52, 61	8, 29, 33, 38, 73

Knowledge of Language (9-14 questions)

Clear and Concise Writing

The ACT will want sentences that are as short and to the point as possible. Clear and concise questions are ONE of the many reasons that PETITE is the strategy for the English test! And remember, Petite is why you go with the shortest answer choice when you don't have any idea on a question!

What is wrong with the following sentence?

Matt was thrilled and delighted to go to the Springsteen Concert!

> For a lot of people, there doesn't appear to be anything wrong with this sentence, but the ACT would see this sentence as being wordy and redundant! "Thrilled" and "delighted" mean the same thing!

Example 10:

> For some people, traditional rock music is <u>associated and connected</u> with screaming musicians and long guitar riffs.

> F. NO CHANGE
> G. connected by some of them
> H. linked by association
> J. associated

> Keep it simple!!! PETITE should be running through your mind on a question like this one! All of the answer choices are wordy and repetitive and say the same thing over and over again (see what I did there!?!?). The correct answer is J.

Example 11:

Among the juniors in high school, prepping for college admission tests has been <u>dreaded for</u> more than a year.

A. NO CHANGE

B. dreaded, one might say, for

C. quite dreaded for

D. dreaded for the duration of

Again, we are looking for the PETITE answer for this question. The shortest answer just happens to be A. NO CHANGE. All of the other choices are way too wordy!

Another thing to keep in mind for clear and concise writing is that the ACT always prefers the active voice is always preferred over the passive voice.

Julie got her hair cut.   OR   A haircut was given to Julie.

Someone or something doing an action is the active voice: Julie got her hair cut.

An action being done to someone or something is passive: A hair cut was given to Julie.

This is confusing sometimes because students will often think that they need to sound "formal" on the ACT because it is a test for college admittance. The complete opposite is true!!! The active voice is ALWAYS preferred!

Practice Problems:

Red Book Test 2	Red Book Test 3	Red Book Test 4	Red Book Test 5
7, 12, 13, 28, 30, 37, 43, 44, 61, 65, 70, 73	7, 13, 17, 26, 39, 40, 71	1, 10, 12, 21, 29, 31, 37, 40, 43, 57, 61, 70, 74	5, 7, 16, 20, 28, 29, 35, 36, 43, 49, 50, 52, 69, 73

Word Choice

There are 1-3 word choice questions on every test. Usually, it is either something that makes sense, or you think they all sounds like they would work. All of the answer choices do have similar meanings, but only ONE answer choice will make sense in the context of the sentence.

Example 12:

It was time to pick the vegetables that he <u>encouraged</u> out of the earth. Which of the following answer choices would best replace the underlined word?

F. pursued
G. coaxed
H. surrendered
J. enlisted

You need think about what all of these words mean in context. Pursued means to chase. Coaxed means to encourage. Surrendered means to give up. Enlisted means to sign up for the armed services. After giving you all these definitions, hopefully you chose G.

Practice Problems:

Red Book Test 2	Red Book Test 3	Red Book Test 4	Red Book Test 5
10, 17, 34, 57, 66, 72	3, 6, 43, 47, 49, 57, 72	9, 17, 24, 26, 35, 42, 54, 55, 60, 64, 69	9, 10, 12, 21, 27, 40

Idioms

Idioms are little bit harder to pin down. Idioms don't have set rules; they are just things that we say in the English language:

"A piece of cake"   "Go bananas"   "eye-catching"

Example 13:

The teacher agreed with Brooke that a person's right <u>for speaking</u> his or her own mind is, in fact, protected by the First Amendment.

 A. NO CHANGE

 B. of speaking

 C. to speak

 D. speaking

On the idiom problems on the test, you just have to go with your gut with what "sounds" right to you. In this case, a right TO do something is the idiom that is being tested, so the only answer that will work is C.

Practice Problems:

Red Book Test 2	Red Book Test 3	Red Book Test 4	Red Book Test 5
18	74	64	9, 11, 14, 37

Commonly Misused Words

Below is a list of words that often show up on the ACT

Accept, Except

 Accept is a verb. (Austin **accepted** the invitation.)
 Except means to leave out. (Everyone was going to the Black Eyed Peas concert **except** for me.)

Affect, Effect

 Affect is an action. (The rain **affected** her hairstyle.)
 Effect is the end result. (His opinion had a great **effect** on my decision)

All right, Alright

 Alright is NOT a word. It is always **all right**.

Between, Among

Between is for two items. (The race **between** Amy and Jenny was close.)
Among is for more than two items. (The scientist is living **among** a group of people.)

Number, Amount

Number is used when you can count items. (A large **number** of students were at the ACT class.)
Amount is used when you cannot count them items. (There was a small **amount** of water in the glass)

Assure, Ensure, Insure

Assure is to guarantee. (I **assure** you that I will not be late.)
Ensure means to make certain. (**Ensure** that the door is locked please!)
Insure means to guard against loss (Please **insure** this package for $100.)

Capital, Capitol

Capital is a place or money. (We went to the **capital** of Illinois, Springfield, to raise **capital** for our new business.)
Capitol is a building. (We went to the **Capitol** building in D.C.)

Compare to, Compare with

Compare to shows a likeness. (I'm often **compared to** my mother.)
Compare with is to look for differences. (The fake was **compared with** the original.)

Complement, Compliment

Complement adds to something. (The dessert **complemented** my meal.)
Compliment is praise. (May was **complimented** on her new shirt.)

Eager, Anxious

Eager is good. (I am **eager** to start my new job!)
Anxious is bad. (I am **anxious** for my Spanish final.)

Farther, Further

> *Farther* is a distance. (Ryan traveled **farther** than I did.)
> *Further* is additional. (We don't expect any **further** delays.)

Fewer, Less

> *Fewer* you can count. (Five **fewer** students went on the trip this year.)
> *Less* you cannot count. (There is **less** air in the front tire.)

Its, It's

> *Its* is possessive. (The dog lost **its** collar.)
> *It's* means it is. (**It's** too bad that your dog ran away.)

Lay, Lie

> *Lay* means to put. (Please **lay** your book on the table.)
> *Lie* means to rest. (Why don't you go **lie** down?)

Learn, Teach

> *Learn* is to gain knowledge. (I have always wanted to **learn** to cook.)
> *Teach* is to give knowledge. (My mom is going to **teach** me to cook.)

Than, Then

> *Than* is a comparison. (I would rather eat chocolate **than** vegetables.)
> *Then* is for time. (I will eat my vegetables, **then** I will eat chocolate.)

That, Which

> *That* is used with info that you need. (This is the book **that** was recommended.)
> *Which* is used with info that you don't need. (That book, **which** is old and tattered, is my favorite.)

Your, You're

> *Your* is possessive. (**Your** brother is going to be late for school.)
> *You're* is you are. (**You're** going to be late too!)

MATH

PLUG

1. IF THE ANSWERS CHOICES ARE NUMBERS, YOU CAN PLUG THE ANSWERS INTO THE PROBLEM (AKA PLUG AND CHUG).
2. IF THE ANSWER CHOICES ARE VARIABLES, PICK A NUMBER TO PLUG INTO THE PROBLEM.

Strategy

Now that we are all done with the English fun, it is time to move on to Math! If you are good at math, you probably already use "plug" on some math questions, but I want to try to show you how to "plug" on problems in a way that you may not have ever thought about before. You can plug your answers into the problems, or you can pick numbers to plug into the problem.

BUT before we dive into these exciting math problems, let's talk about the overall strategy for math.

Again, keep an eye out for these reminders for hints and strategy examples!

> ## Game Plan for Math
>
> 1. Underline what the question is asking for.
> 2. Take notes or draw a picture.
> 3. Solve the problem using your math skills or "plugging."

1. Read the question and underline what the question is asking for.

It is SOOO easy to start reading a math question and *think* you know what the question is asking for, which is why it is SOOOO important to make sure you know what the question is asking.

Example 1. What is 32% of $20.10 to the nearest dollar?
- A. $6.00
- B. $6.43
- C. $7.00
- D. $64.00
- E. $643.00

For Example 1, it is incredibly easy to read just the beginning of the problem and jump right in to solve the problem! If you did that, you probably picked B as the answer. If you picked E, you simply forgot that when multiplying in a percent problem, you need to change the percent to a decimal. Now, if you read the entire question, you noticed the *to the nearest dollar* at the end of the question; this means that you need to round the answer. A is the correct answer.

2. Take notes or draw a picture.

This might sound like a weird concept when you are working on a math problem.

Why would you want to take notes?!?! On word problems, "taking notes" will help you pull out the information that you need in order to solve the problem.

Draw a picture?!?!? If you come across a problem that is describing a shape or a picture, it will help you to visualize what the problem is talking about by drawing a picture.

3. **Solve the problem.**

   a. **Use your math skills.**

   If you know what to do, go for it! Don't forget to double check that you are answering what the question is asking!

   b. **If you are stuck, ask yourself, "Is there a way that you can use the answer choices to help?"**

   This is where "plug" comes into play! There are two times that you can plug on the math problems. You can plug answers into the problem when there are numbers as answer choices:

   Example 2. If $\dfrac{2x}{7} = \dfrac{x-2}{3}$, which of the following does x equal?

   F.   –14

   G.   –2

   H.   2

   J.   7

   (K.)   14

   $$\frac{2x}{7} = \frac{x-2}{3}$$
   $$6x = 7(x-2)$$
   $$6x = 7x - 14$$
   $$-7x \quad -7x$$
   $$-x = -14$$
   $$\frac{-x}{-1} = \frac{-14}{-1}$$
   $$x = 14$$

   If you know how to do this problem (cross multiplying), go for it! If you aren't sure how to solve this problem, it is the perfect opportunity to use the first way to "plug" our answer choices! The question asks "what does x equal?" which tells us that you can plug the answer choices directly in for x. When you plug in the numbers, you want to start with the middle answer choice. That way, if the number is too big, you can move on to the smaller answer choices, but if it is too small, you can move on to the bigger answer choices. In other words, starting in the middle can save you time! If we plug

   H(2) into the problem, you will get: $\dfrac{2(2)}{7} = \dfrac{2-2}{3}$ and when you do the math,

   $\dfrac{4}{7} \neq \dfrac{0}{3}$ Obviously, H is not the correct answer, so try another one! I don't

   like negative numbers, so I would try J(7) next: $\dfrac{2(7)}{7} = \dfrac{7-2}{3} \rightarrow 2 \neq \dfrac{5}{3}$ J is out

   now too! Let's try K(14): $\dfrac{2(14)}{7} = \dfrac{14-2}{3} \rightarrow 4 = 4$ We found the right answer –

   K!   the longer process would be to plug in the answers to find the correct answer if I was stuck.

So now what do you do if you don't have numbers in your answer choices? There is still a way to "plug" answer choices. If there are variables in the answer choices, you can pick a number to plug in!!

Example 3. Which of the following is a factored form of the expression $5x^2 - 13x - 6$?

A. $(x-3)(5x+2)$

B. $(x-2)(5x-3)$

C. $(x-2)(5x+3)$

D. $(x+2)(5x-3)$

E. $(x+3)(5x-2)$

$5x^2 - 13x - 6$

$(x-3)(5x+2)$

$5x^2 + 2x - 15x - 6$

$5x^2 + -13x - 6$

When you have variables in your answer choices, you can "plug" a number in. So, let's plug in the number 2. I'm going to plug 2 into the original problem: $5(2)^2 - 13(2) - 6 = 5(4) - 26 - 6 = -12$ Now I'm going to plug 2 into the answer choices to see which answer gives me -12!

A. $(2-3)(5(2)+2) = (-1)(12) = -12$

B. $(2-2)(5(2)-3) = (0)(7) = 0$

C. $(2-2)(5(2)+3) = (0)(13) = 0$

D. $(2+2)(5(2)-3) = (4)(7) = 28$

E. $(2+3)(5(2)-2) = (5)(8) = 40$

A has to be the right answer! It is the only choice that matched the problem! If I had two answers that matched, all I would do is pick another number to plug in.

Try to stay away from picking 0 or 1 because they have special properties. If you know how to solve the problem, go for it, but picking numbers is a fast way to check and make sure you got the right answer!

Math Timing/Scoring

It is important to keep in mind the timing for the math section. This is probably the easiest part of the test to keep track of time because you have approximately one minute per problem. Some important tips to keep in mind:

- The math section is the ONLY part of the test that has the general trend of easy to hard.

  If you struggle with math:
- Focus on the first 40 questions.
- Doing well on the first 40, and trying your best on the remaining 20 (or guessing the same letter if you need to) can result in a **<u>26!</u>**
  - o Try to use your answer choices AS MUCH AS POSSIBLE!

If you scored in the high 20s on your first practice test in math, but struggled with timing, my expert advice is to try doing the math test backwards.

  - o I would NEVER attempt this strategy for the first time on an ACTUAL ACT test.
  - o What might happen for you is that you will have more time to look at the harder problems, which you have a better chance of getting when you aren't tired and pressed for time.
  - o You then are forced to move through the easier problems at the beginning of the test faster than you might have originally.
  - o If you try this, you will either LOVE it or HATE it. I have found that there is no in between for this strategy. This is exactly why you need to practice it!

Integrating Essential Skills (24-26 questions)

Basic Operations

Another part of basic operations is simply arithmetic, and an important part of that is order of operations. You may or may not have heard of "Please excuse my dear Aunt Sally," but this is an acronym for the order of operations.

 TI-84 Tip: To do fractions on your calculator, choose "Alpha" then "Y=" and you should see the button that says n/d or U_n_d. You can use this to see a fraction the way that you write it!

Please Excuse My Dear Aunt Sally

$$6 - 1(0) \dot{+} 2^3/(2+2)$$

Parentheses need to be done first.   (2+2)

$$6 - 1(0) + 2^3/(2+2) = 6 - 1(0) + 2^3/(4)$$

Exponents are next. 2^3

$$6 - 1(0) + 2^3/(2+2) = 6 - 1(0) + 8/(4)$$

Multiplication and **D**ivision follow.   1(0) and 8/4

$$6 - 1(0) + 8/(4) = 6 - 0 + 2$$

Addition and **S**ubtraction are last! 6-0+2

$$6 - 0 + 2 = 8$$

And now it is time for a fraction refresher!!! When adding and subtracting fractions, you need to get common denominators first.

$$\frac{1}{3} + \frac{1}{4} = \frac{4}{12} + \frac{3}{12} = \frac{7}{12}$$

When multiplying fractions, you can just multiply across. For division, you need to multiply by the reciprocal (you need to flip the second fraction!).

$$\frac{1}{3}\left(\frac{1}{4}\right) = \frac{1}{12} \qquad\qquad \frac{1}{3} \div \frac{1}{4} = \frac{1}{3}\left(\frac{4}{1}\right) = \frac{4}{3}$$

Example 4. Brooke ran $2\frac{1}{2}$ miles on Saturday and $4\frac{2}{5}$ miles on Sunday. How much did she run over the weekend?

F. $6\frac{1}{2}$

G. $6\frac{3}{8}$

H. $6\frac{3}{7}$

J. $6\frac{9}{10}$

K. $6\frac{1}{10}$

$2\frac{1}{2}$ saturday $4\frac{2}{5}$ sunday

$2+4=6$

$\frac{(5\times1)}{(5\times2)}+\frac{(2\times2)}{(5\times2)}$

$\frac{5}{10}+\frac{4}{10}=\frac{9}{10}$

$6+\frac{9}{10}=6\frac{9}{10}$

The easiest way to solve this problem is using the tip for your calculator! Or you can do the math by hand… add the units (2+4=6) and then get common denominators $\frac{1}{2}+\frac{2}{5}=\frac{5}{10}+\frac{4}{10}=\frac{9}{10}$ J is the correct answer.

Practice Problems:

Red Book Test 2	Red Book Test 3	Red Book Test 4	Red Book Test 5
3, 18, 37, 58	4, 7, 9, 13, 19, 30, 48	4, 10, 11, 14, 16, 17, 57	4, 5, 21, 28, 41

Scientific Notation

Scientific notation is rewriting a number with one digit in front of the decimal point, and then counting the number of decimal places and writing that as a factor of 10.

You move the decimal point to the right for positive exponents (a positive exponent is a BIG number) and to the left for negative exponents (a negative exponent is a really SMALL number).

What is 235,000,000,000 in scientific notation? 2.35×10^{11}
11 10 9 8 7 6 5 4 3 2 1

How would you write out the number 6.9×10^{-5}? 0.000069
1 2 3 4 5

Practice Problems:

Red Book Test 2	Red Book Test 3	Red Book Test 4	Red Book Test 5
None	16	None	None

Factors & Multiples

A **factor** is a number that divides exactly into a larger number.

What are the factors of 24? 1, 2, 3, 4, 6, 8, 12, 24

7 would not be a factor of 24 because there is a remainder when you do the division.

A **multiple** is what you get when you multiply two numbers together.

What are the first five multiples of 7? 7, 14, 21, 28, 35

A **prime** number has only two factors, itself and one.

Is 1 a prime number? No, because it only has one factor: 1.

Is 2 a prime number? Yes, because it has only two factors: 1,2 – and it is special because it is the *only* even number that is prime.

What are the prime numbers less than 20? 2, 3, 5, 7, 11, 13, 17, 19

Example 5: Which of the following lists all the positive factors of 8?

A. 1, 8
B. 2, 4
C. 2, 4, 6
D. 8, 16, 32
E. 1, 2, 4, 8

Hopefully this is an easy problem after the definition you just got!! The correct answer is E. If you chose A or B, you didn't list ALL of the positive factors. If you chose D, you got multiples and factors confused.

Greatest Common Factor is the BIGGEST number that goes IN evenly to all of the numbers.

What is the greatest common factor of 60, 24, and 18? The easiest way to figure this out is to look at the factors of the smallest number, 18: 1, 2, 3, 6, 9, 18.

Does 18 go into 60 and 24? No. Does 9 go into 60 and 24? No. Does 6? Yes!! That is your answer. 6 is the greatest common factor of 60, 24, and 18.

Example 6. For all positive integers x, what is the greatest common factor of the two numbers $216x$ and $180x$?

F. 6
G. 72
H. x
J. $12x$
K. $36x$

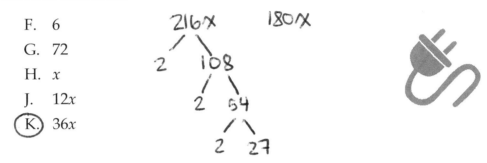

If you don't want to use the method that I just discussed to solve this problem, you can "plug" your answer choices! Since it is asking for the GREATEST, you would want to start with the largest answer choices. Does $36x$ go into $216x$ and $180x$ evenly? It does! You have your answer choice K.

Least Common Multiple is the SMALLEST number that all of the numbers go INTO.

We use this concept to get the common denominator in fractions!

What is the least common multiple of 4, 5, and 6? Now you want to use the largest number, and look at the multiples of it! 6, 12, 18, 24, 30, 36, 42, 48, 54, 60 and try to find the smallest number that 4 and 5 go into. In this case, the first number that all 3 divide into evenly is 60.

Example 7. What is the least common denominator when adding the fractions
$\frac{x}{4}, \frac{y}{6}, \frac{z}{20}$?

    A.   20
    B.   24
    C.   40
    D.   60
    E.   120

Again, if you don't want to solve this problem the way that we just did, you can use your answer choices. Since it is asking for the LEAST common denominator, you want to start with the smallest answer choices. Do 4, 6, and 20 all divide evenly into 20? No. 24? No. 40? No. 60? Yes! There is your answer! D.

Practice Problems:

Red Book Test 2	Red Book Test 3	Red Book Test 4	Red Book Test 5
None	12	47	None

Remainders

A remainder is what is left over when you divide numbers. You might remember the "old school" way of determining remainders:

$$\begin{array}{r} 5 \\ 5\overline{)27} \\ -25 \\ \hline 2 \end{array}$$ so the reminder is 2 because that is what is left over!

The way that this shows up on the test is probably different than how you have ever worked with remainders in the past. The problem involves some sort of pattern: possibly a repeating decimal.

Example 8. What is the 95ᵗʰ digit of the decimal $0.\overline{258}$?

F. 2

G. 5

H. 8

J. 9

K. 3

To figure out this problem, we need to apply the principle of remainders. You count how long your repeating pattern is (in this case it is 3 digits long). Then we divide 95 by how long the pattern is (3).

$$\begin{array}{r} 31 \\ 3\overline{)95} \\ -93 \\ \hline 2 \end{array}$$ The remainder is 2. If the remainder is 1, the answer would

be the first digit in the pattern (2). If the remainder is 2, the answer will be the second digit in the patter (5), and if the remainder is 0, then the answer will be the third digit. So in this case, the answer is G (5).

If this remainder problem freaks you out a little bit, no worries. This doesn't appear on the test very often!

Practice Problems:

Red Book Test 2	Red Book Test 3	Red Book Test 4	Red Book Test 5
46	None	45	None

Ratios and Proportions

The easiest way to work through ratio problems is by setting up a table. Let's work through an example:

In Anisha's class, the ratio of boys to girls is 1 to 3. If there are 32 students in the class, how many girls are there?

Start by labeling the rows, and then fill in the information that you know. There is 1 boy for every 3 girls.

Boys	Girls	Total
1	3	

How many total? You add going across the rows.

Boys	Girls	Total
1	3	**4**

Now, write the other information you are given in the question in the second row.

Boys	Girls	Total
1	3	4
		32

You multiply to get from the first row to the second row (4 times 8 is 32). So then you multiply the other numbers by 8 to fill in the second row.

Boys	Girls	Total
1	3	4
8	**24**	32

Now you can answer whatever the question is!

How many girls are in Anisha's class?   24 girls

You can also solve the same problem by setting up the ratios as fractions. This is known as a proportion. Try setting up the problem about Anisha's class as a proportion:

$\dfrac{3\,girls}{4\,total} = \dfrac{x\,girls}{32\,total}$ How do you solve a problem when two fractions are equal to each

other?

You cross multiply.

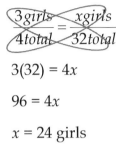

$3(32) = 4x$

$96 = 4x$

$x = 24$ girls

Either way, you will get the same answer – it just may be easier to set up the table!

Example 9. In Grace's math class, the ratio of Juniors to Seniors is 3:5. If there is a total of 1200 students in the Junior and Senior classes, how many more Seniors are there?

A. 2

B. 300

C. 450

D. 750

E. 1200

Juniors	Seniors	Total
3	5	**8**
		1200

8 times what is 1200? 150! So we need to multiply 3 and 5 by 150.

Juniors	Seniors	Total
3	5	8
400	**750**	**1200**

But now to get the answer, we need to answer what the question is asking… how many more seniors are there? 750-400 is 300! The answer is B.

Practice Problems:

Red Book Test 2	Red Book Test 3	Red Book Test 4	Red Book Test 4
1, 7	1, 28	13, 15, 17, 34, 36	14, 17, 21, 24, 29

Rates

Rates are used for several reasons in math. The slope of a graph can be considered rate. When the word "per" appears in a problem, you can consider it a rate. The easiest way to think about rate problems is considering them a type of ratio – you just need to make sure the units match up!

How many minutes are in 2 days?

$$\left(\frac{2\ days}{}\right)\left(\frac{24\ hours}{1\ days}\right)\left(\frac{60\ minutes}{1\ hour}\right) = 2{,}880\ minutes$$

Practice Problems:

Red Book Test 2	Red Book Test 3	Red Book Test 4	Red Book Test 5
45	None	None	34, 30

Percent

Percent problems are so much easier when you realize how to use the wording of the question to help you set up the equation.

Of means multiply. Is means equals.

It is also important to note that in percent problems, you need to turn a percent (like 30%) into a decimal in order to use it in the problems. You can think of it as moving the decimal over two places or as dividing by 100, but either way, you will get 0.30 in this example.

To get the percent increase or decrease, divide the difference by the original amount.

$$\frac{Original - New}{Original}$$ Positive number is increasing   Negative number is decreasing

And the last bit of advice for percent problems is that when they don't give you a number to work with, this is the perfect opportunity to "plug" (see Example 10!!)

Example 10. A number is increased by 25% and the resulting number is then decreased by 20%. The final number is what percent of the original number?

F. 90%
G. 95%
H. 100%
J. 105%
K. 120%

Like I already mentioned, this best this to do on the problem is to "plug" in a number, and the easiest number to plug in on percent problems is 100!!!! So let me read the problem after plugging in 100: A number (100) is increased by 25% (so that means 100 times 0.25 = 25). If the number 100 in increased by 25, our new number is 125. Now the problem says the resulting number (125) is decreased by 20% (125 times 0.20 = 25), and since it is decreased, we need to subtract 125-25 = 100. The last part of the question says the final number (which we got to be 100) is what percent of the original number (100)? The answer is 100%, or choice H.

Plug in 100 when doing percent problems!

Practice Problems:

Red Book Test 2	Red Book Test 3	Red Book Test 4	Red Book Test 5
15, 60	15, 22, 50	9, 40	59

Combining Terms, Simplification, and Rearrangement

You are likely so used to combing terms, simplifying, and rearranging, that you don't even think about it as you work through problems. If you are comfortable with Algebra, these are probably very straightforward problems for you. If you don't like Algebra, these are VERY easy problems to use the "plug" strategy on. REMEMBER: In an Algebra problem, what you do to one side of the equation, you should do to the other!

$\dfrac{2x-4}{3} = x$ You can multiply both sides of the equation by 3.

$2x - 4 = 3x$ Now you would subtract $2x$ from both sides of the equation.

$-4 = x$ You are done!

Example 11. The expression 2(x-(y-z)) is equivalent to which of the following?

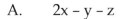
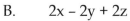

A. 2x – y – z
B. 2x – 2y + 2z
C. 2x – 2y – 2z
D. 2x – y + z
E. 2x + 2y + 2z

If you aren't sure how to approach this problem, "plug!" You can pick values for x, y, and z! For example, x=1, y=2, and z=3. So now I have 2(1-(2-3)) and when I simplify this, I would get 2(1-(-1)) = 2(2) = 4. Now I would plug the same values of x, y, and z into the answer choices to see which answer choice gives me 4. It is faster to solve by just rewriting the expression with the variables in it, but it is more important that you get the right answer! In this case, the correct answer is B. If you got C, you didn't distribute the negative sign to both the y and the z.

Practice Problems:

Red Book Test 2	Red Book Test 3	Red Book Test 4	Red Book Test 5
12, 28	21, 39	7, 37	37, 43

Probability

Almost all probability problems boil down to one thing:

$$\frac{\text{Desired outcome}}{\text{Total number of outcomes}}$$

It is important to note that probability must be greater than zero and less than or equal to one.

If the probability that Kelsey will win the state cheerleading competition is 0.7, what is the probability that she will not win? It would be 0.3 because they need to add up to be 1.

Think about probability as [what you are looking for] over [the total number of possibilities].

Example 12. A bag contains 6 red marbles, 5 yellow marbles, and 7 green marbles. What is the probability of NOT choosing a red marble?

F. $\dfrac{1}{3}$

G. $\dfrac{5}{18}$

H. $\dfrac{7}{18}$

J. $\dfrac{13}{18}$

K. $\dfrac{2}{3}$

To solve the problem, we want to figure out the desired outcome (NOT choosing a red marble) and divide it by the total number of outcomes (all of the marbles). If we do not choose a red marble, then we have a yellow or a green marble. We need to add those together (5+7 = 12). To figure out the total number of marbles, we need to add all of the colors together (5+7+6 = 18). Now the last step is to divide $\dfrac{12}{18} = \dfrac{2}{3}$, so K is the correct answer.

Practice Problems:

Red Book Test 2	Red Book Test 3	Red Book Test 4	Red Book Test 5
4, 41	29, 33, 60	2, 26, 38, 39, 49	1, 42

Pictograms, Tables, Charts

You will have two tables or graphs on the math section with 2-4 questions asking about information in the figure. Now when we get to the science section, we will have a different strategy for looking at the tables and charts, but on the math section, you NEED to read the information about the table or graph. They usually give you information that will help you answer the questions. In fact, it is usually difficult to get the correct answer without reading what is written! So after you read, you want to quickly look over the figure before going to the questions.

Practice Problems:

Red Book Test 2	Red Book Test 3
None	33, 34, 35, 50, 51, 52

Mean, Median, Mode

Mean is the same thing as the average. To get the mean (average), you add up all the numbers, and then divide by how many numbers you added.

What is the average of 2, 6, 9, 11? $\dfrac{2+6+9+11}{4} = \dfrac{28}{4} = 7$

To find the **median**, you start by putting the numbers in order. Then the median is the number in the middle – just like the median on a highway!

What is the median of 2, 8, 4, 12, 7, 5, 20?   2, 4, 5, 7, 8, 12, 20   Median is 7!

If you have an even set of numbers, you take the average of the two numbers in the middle.

The **mode** is the number that appears the **most** often!

What is the mode of 4, 8, 8, 12, 16? 8

Example 13. To determine a student's overall test score for the semester, Ms. Wiles throws out the lowest test score and takes the average of the remaining test scores. Lisa earned the following test scores in Ms. Wiles' class this semester: 62, 78, 83, 84, and 93. What overall test score did Lisa earn in Ms. Wiles' class this semester?

A. 67.6

B. 80.0

C. 83.0

D. 83.5

E. 84.5

Make sure you read this question carefully! You need to throw out the lowest score: 62. So now when you add them up (78 + 83 + 84 + 93 = 338), you only divide by 4: 338/4 = 84.5 which is answer E. If you got choice B, then you didn't throw out the lowest score.

Example 14. What is the median of the following 7 scores? 42, 67, 33, 79, 33, 89, 21

F. 42

G. 52

H. 54.5

J. 56

K. 79

After you put these scores in order from lowest to highest: 21, 33, 33, 42, 67, 79, 89, then figure out which one is in the middle, you should get 42, or choice F, as the correct answer.

Practice Problems:

Red Book Test 2	Red Book Test 3	Red Book Test 4	Red Book Test 5
5, 29	2, 35	23, 41	22, 25, 39, 50, 56

Substitution

Substitute means "to put in place of another"; so when you substitute, you just plug in! The thing that you need to keep in mind on these problems is that it is extremely common for these problems to involve negative signs – SO BE CAREFUL!!! For this reason, I recommend plugging the numbers into the problems in parentheses.

Example 15: What is the value of the expression $(x - y)^2$ when x = 5 and y = -1?

   A.   4
   B.   6
   C.   16
   D.   24
   E.   36

Like I recommended, plug the numbers into the problem using parentheses. $((5) - (-1))^2 = (5 + 1)^2 = 6^2 = 36$ choice E. If you got C, that means you forgot to make the double negative a positive. Hopefully, these will be really straightforward questions for you.

If you aren't sure whether or not you need to use () in your calculator, use them just in case!

Practice Problems:

Red Book Test 2	Red Book Test 3	Red Book Test 4	Red Book Test 5
23, 32, 35, 44	3, 6, 11, 31	21	3, 10, 18, 20

Word Problems

My first piece of advice for word problems is to take notes. Word problems can be very overwhelming… so many words, and it is easy to not want to read!! What happens when you take notes is you will pull the information out of the problem that you need to solve it.

Math Translation Help

What words represent addition?

more, more than, in addition

Subtraction?

fewer, less than, difference,

Multiplication?

times, of, product

Division?

per, divided by

Equals?

is, equals, equivalent

Example 16. Which of the following mathematical expressions is equivalent to the verbal expression "A number, x, squared is 39 more than the product of 10 and x"?

F. $2x = 39 + 10x$

G. $2x = 39x + 10x$

H. $x^2 = 39 - 10x$

J. $x^2 = 39 + x^{10}$

K. $x^2 = 39 + 10x$

The problem starts off by saying "x squared is" so the problem needs to start off with x^2 so I can eliminate choices F and G. "39 more than" means addition, so I can eliminate H. "Product of 10 and x" means multiplication… so the correct choice is K!

Practice Problems:

Red Book Test 2	Red Book Test 3	Red Book Test 4	Red Book Test 5
2, 3, 13, 14, 15, 18, 21, 27, 37, 46, 58	7, 13, 15, 19, 30, 37, 42, 45, 50, 52, 56	2, 3, 4, 5, 11, 16, 22, 24, 26, 36, 39, 40, 41, 49, 51, 54, 55, 57	5, 6, 11, 20, 21, 22, 26, 27, 28, 32, 33, 34, 35, 36, 38, 39, 40, 44, 50, 54, 57, 59

Preparing for Higher Math (34-36 questions)

Number & Quantity (4-6 questions)

Real Number System

Let's start off with a review of some vocabulary! There are very rarely questions that test you on what these words mean, but there are many questions that use the vocabulary if you know what it means. Below are the definitions and examples.

Natural numbers are the counting numbers NOT including zero: 1, 2, 3, etc.

Whole numbers are the counting numbers (including 0) you learned as a kid: 1,9

Integers are the whole numbers and their negatives: -28, -7, 23

Rational numbers are numbers that can be written as a fraction: $\frac{7}{3}, -\frac{1}{10}, -0.63$

Irrational numbers are numbers that can**not** be written as a fraction: $\pi, \sqrt{3}, e$

Real numbers are all of the above! The only non-real number that you will see on the test are called complex numbers (you might know them as imaginary or complex numbers i).

Practice Problems:

Red Book Test 2	Red Book Test 3	Red Book Test 4	Red Book Test 5
17, 31, 39, 40, 49	4, 27, 32	37, 58	1, 31, 37, 48, 53, 55, 60

Complex Numbers

Complex numbers are numbers that use i. These questions are not common on the ACT. In fact, there is a good chance that you won't have an imaginary numbers question at all. If you do, you will always be given the fact that $i^2 = -1$.

There is a pattern that emerges when you look at imaginary numbers:

$i = i$

$i^2 = -1$

$i^3 = (i)(i^2) = i(-1) = -i$

$i^4 = (i^2)(i^2) = (-1)(-1) = 1$

When you have a problem that looks like distributing, that is exactly what you need to do.

$(2i+1)(i-3) = 2i^2 - 6i + i - 3 = 2i^2 - 5i - 3 = 2(-1) - 5i - 3 = -5 - 5i$

There is an i button on your calculator,. On the TI-84, it is 2nd and the decimal point.

Example 17. Given that $i^2 = -1$, simplify the following: $\dfrac{2}{(1+i)} \cdot \dfrac{(1-i)}{(1-i)} = ?$

A. $\dfrac{2-i}{1-i}$

B. $\dfrac{2-2i}{1+i}$

C. $\dfrac{2-2i}{1}$

D. $(1+i)$

E. $(1-i)$

To solve this problem, you need to distribute. If you don't understand anything with the "i"s, you can still get a 50/50 shot on this problem just by looking at the numerator. $2(1-i) = 2 - 2i$, which means that only B or C can be the correct answer. I could even just guess that C would be the correct answer because if I need to multiply the denominators, I wouldn't have (1-*i*) in the denominator anymore. And look at that, C is the correct answer. If you don't believe me, try distributing like I did in the problem above: Example 17.

Another common topic that will appear with complex (imaginary) number is the idea of conjugates. It is based on the idea of the difference of two squares. When I multiply $(x + 3)(x - 3)$ something magical takes place.

$$(x + 3)(x - 3) = x^2 - 3x + 3x - 9 = x^2 - 9$$

The middle term disappears! We can use the concept for imaginary numbers too! When the middle term disappears, we can get rid of the *i* term!

$$(x + 3i)(x - 3i) = x^2 - 3xi + 3xi - 3i^2 = x^2 - 9i^2 = x^2 - 9(-1) = x^2 + 9$$

So all that silly word "conjugate" means is that you have the same numbers/variables in both sets of parentheses, but you have different signs. Then when you multiply them out, the middle term cancels out.

Practice Problems:

Red Book Test 2	Red Book Test 3	Red Book Test 4	Red Book Test 5
39, 56	41, 58	58	60

Vectors

Something new has come to the ACT recently, and it sounds scary. Vectors look like funny parentheses < > and IRL (in real life for those of you that don't speak text) they are usually used in physics or flying (like for a pilot). Vectors are different from just normal points on a graph because they have magnitude and direction. Now with all that set, doing vector math is straightforward.

You can add or subtract vectors by combining numbers that are in the same locations in the vectors:

$$\langle 2,4 \rangle + \langle -1,9 \rangle = \langle 2 - 1, 4 + 9 \rangle = \langle 1,13 \rangle$$

You can also multiply into a vector – distribute (multiply) first and then add:

$$3\langle 4,2\rangle - 2\langle 7,-3\rangle = \langle 3(4), 3(2)\rangle + \langle -2(7), -2(-3)\rangle$$

$$= \langle 12,6\rangle + \langle -14,6\rangle = \langle 12 - 14, 6 + 6\rangle = \langle -2,12\rangle$$

Practice Problems:

Red Book Test 2	Red Book Test 3	Red Book Test 4	Red Book Test 5
57	54	None	None

Matrices

You can only add matrices that have the same number of rows and columns. To add matrices, you add numbers that are in the same locations.

$$\begin{bmatrix} 3 & 6 \\ 2 & 7 \end{bmatrix} + \begin{bmatrix} 6 & 1 \\ 13 & 5 \end{bmatrix} = \begin{bmatrix} 3+6 & 6+1 \\ 2+13 & 7+5 \end{bmatrix} = \begin{bmatrix} 9 & 7 \\ 15 & 12 \end{bmatrix}$$

If there are coefficients (numbers) in front of the matrices, you distribute them to every number in the matrix.

$$-3\begin{bmatrix} 4 & -8 \\ 5 & 2 \end{bmatrix} = \begin{bmatrix} -12 & 24 \\ -15 & -6 \end{bmatrix}$$

The ACT might ask you to multiply matrices. This would be considered one of the most difficult questions on the test. You multiply row by column:

When you multiply matrices, write out the sizes of the matrices you are multiplying: the first number is the number of rows, and the second number is the number of columns. If I have 3 rows and 2 columns, it is a (3 X 2) matrix.

In order to multiply, the middle numbers need to match, and the result is the outside numbers. Very confusing – until I show you a shortcut!

(3 X 2) x (2 x 4): The 2s in the middle are the same, so I can multiply them! The answer will be the outside numbers: (3 x 4)

Can you multiply a $(3X2)x(3X3)$?   Nope – the 2 and the 3 in the middle don't match

a $(4X3)x(3X2)$?   Yup – the 3's match. The answer will be a (4 x 2).

Now it can be a little confusing when you multiply matrices. You can do this on your calculator, but let me walk through one example. You need to think row by column. It might help to watch a YouTube video.

$$\begin{bmatrix} 1 & 2 \\ 3 & 4 \end{bmatrix} \times \begin{bmatrix} 5 & 6 \\ 7 & 8 \end{bmatrix} = \begin{bmatrix} (1)(5)+(2)(7) & (1)(6)+(2)(8) \\ (3)(5)+(4)(7) & (3)(6)+(4)(8) \end{bmatrix} = \begin{bmatrix} 19 & 22 \\ 43 & 50 \end{bmatrix}$$

Example 18. $\begin{bmatrix} 2 & -2 \\ -1 & 3 \end{bmatrix} - \begin{bmatrix} 0 & 1 \\ -1 & 2 \end{bmatrix} = ?$

Rows across

C down
O
L
U
M
N

F. $\begin{bmatrix} 2 & -3 \\ 0 & 1 \end{bmatrix}$

G. $\begin{bmatrix} 2 & -1 \\ -2 & 5 \end{bmatrix}$

H. $\begin{bmatrix} 1 & -2 \\ -2 & 1 \end{bmatrix}$

J. $\begin{bmatrix} 2 & -1 \\ 0 & 1 \end{bmatrix}$

K. $\begin{bmatrix} 2 & -3 \\ -2 & 1 \end{bmatrix}$

You can work through the problem while eliminating answer choices. The top left number needs to be 2 (because 2+0), so you can eliminate choice H. -2 – 1 = -3, so the upper right number needs to be -3. Now we are only left with F and K. $-1-(-1) = -1+1 = 0$ which means the bottom left is 0, so the answer has to be F.

There will only be one matrix problem, if there is any at all, so no need to worry if you have no idea what I am talking about here!

Practice Problems:

Red Book Test 2	Red Book Test 3	Red Book Test 4	Red Book Test 5
42	None	60	15

Exponents

Let's review exponent rules! When you are adding or subtracting, you can only combine terms that are the same: $x^2 + x^2 = 2x^2$

When you are multiplying, you add the exponents: $\qquad (x^3)(x^2) = (xxx)(xx) = x^5$

You subtract when you are dividing $\dfrac{x^4}{x^2} = \dfrac{xxxx}{xx} = x^2$

When you raise a power to a power, you multiply: $\quad (x^2)^4 = (xx)^4 = (xxxxxxxx) = x^8$

What does a negative in the exponent do? It flips the exponent to the denominator

$$x^{-3} = \dfrac{1}{x^3}$$

When there is a fraction in the exponent, it is the same as taking the root of something.

$$x^{\frac{1}{2}} = \sqrt{x}$$

The number in the numerator goes under the root, and the number in the denominator goes on the outside of the root.

$$x^{\frac{3}{4}} = \sqrt[4]{x^3}$$

Example 19: If $3^x = 54$, then which of the following must be true?

        A. $1 < x < 2$
        B. $2 < x < 3$
        C. $3 < x < 4$
        D. $4 < x < 5$
        E . $5 < x$

This problem can be solved mathematically by taking the log of both sides, but it is easier to solve if you "plug" in your answer choices.

$3^1=3$ $3^2=9$ $3^3=27$ $3^4=81$... I don't need to go any further. Since 54 falls between 27 and 81, the answer has to be C.

Practice Problems:

Red Book Test 2	Red Book Test 3	Red Book Test 4	Red Book Test 5
36	48, 52, 55	27, 33	41

Logarithms

Logs are the inverse of exponents. There are some buttons on your TI-84 calculator that make logs easy. I will share the formulas, in case you don't have a graphing calculator.

The easiest way I have to remember logs is using the anacronym BAE (which I have been using for years – long before it meant boyfriend or girlfriend!) BAE stands for:

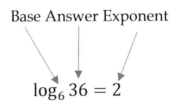

$$\log_6 36 = 2$$

So, if I rewrote this as an exponential problem, it would be $6^2 = 36$. The base is 6, the exponent is 2, and the answer is 36.

The log button on your calculator can only be used if the base is 10. Here is the formula you would need to solve this:

$$\frac{\log(36)}{\log(6)} = 2$$

It is "log of the number in the large font divided by the log of the number in the small font," and if you solve the problem like this, you can use the log on your calculator.

 *On the TI-84, there is an option on the Math menu for logBASE, and it will make the log look like it is written out in the BAE example above.*

Harder log problems might ask about expanding or condensing log problems. I'm going to quickly go over a couple of rules.

- Expanding a log problem
  - Bring exponents down in front.
  - If the "answers" are being multiplied, you can change those to addition.
  - If the "answers' are being divided, you can change those to subtraction.

$$\log\left(\frac{3x}{4}\right)^2 = 2\left(\log\left(\frac{3x}{4}x\right)\right) = 2(\log(3) + \log(x) - \log(4))$$

- Condensing a log problem (complete opposite of the problem above)
  - Put coefficients up as exponents.
  - Addition turns into multiplication.
  - Subtraction turns into division.

Practice Problems:

Red Book Test 2	Red Book Test 3	Red Book Test 4	Red Book Test 5
59	49	35, 53	46

Algebra (7-9 questions)

Distribution

When you have parentheses, you usually need to distribute.

$$4(x+5) = 4x + 20 \quad \text{OR} \quad (2x)^2 = 2^2 x^2 = 4x^2$$

However, it is different when you have two terms in the parentheses:

A way to remember what to do is the term FOIL – First Outer Inner Last

$$(x+2)(2x+3) = 2x^2 + 3x + 4x + 6 = 2x^2 + 7x + 6$$

If you have a squared term (like below), it is going to be easier to see what to do if you write out the term twice. Then you can FOIL!

$$(x+2)^2 = (x+2)(x+2) = x^2 + 2x + 2x + 4 = x^2 + 4x + 4$$

Example 20: Which of the following is equivalent to $(4x^2)^3$?

F. $4x^5$

G. $12x^5$

H. $12x^6$

J. $64x^5$

K. $64x^6$

You can either apply the rules of exponents to this problem:

$$(4^1 x^2)^3 = (4^3 x^6) = 64x^6$$

OR you can "plug" in a number... say x=2

$(4 \cdot 2^2)^3 = (4 \cdot 4)^3 = 16^3 = 4,096$ and now "plug" x=2 into each of the answer choices to see which answer matches:

F. 128
G. 384
H. 768
J. 2,048
K. 4,096

Either way, K is the answer!

Practice Problems:

Red Book Test 2	Red Book Test 3	Red Book Test 4	Red Book Test 5
12	9, 21	58	None

Factoring

Factoring means taking out what is common:

$$15x^5 - 10x^3 + 10x^2 = 10x^2(3x^3 - 2x + 1)$$

Factoring for quadratic equations ($ax^2 + bx + c$) is reverse FOIL

You multiply to get the first number, add to get the second, and multiply to get the third.

To remember this, think MAM and MA!

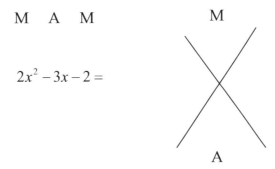

You multiply the two M numbers (2 and -2) and put it where the M is, and put the A number where the A is.

Now, think about what multiplies to be -4 and adds to be -3

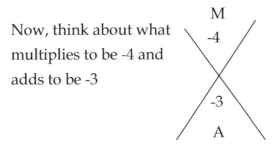

-4 and 1

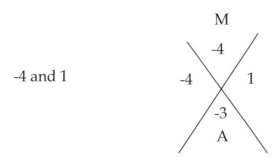

You start by leaving the first and last terms alone and splitting the middle term into the numbers that we came up with. Then you factor by grouping.

$$2x^2 - 3x - 2 =$$
$$2x^2 - 4x + 1x - 2 =$$
$$(2x^2 - 4x) + (1x - 2) =$$
$$2x(x - 4) + 1(x - 4) =$$
$$(x - 4)(2x + 1) =$$

Practice Problems:

Red Book Test 2	Red Book Test 3	Red Book Test 4	Red Book Test 5
9, 28	58	None	None

Symbolism

Symbolism problems do not appear often, but when they do, they are really straightforward.

Example 21: If (A# B) = 3A-2B, then (2 # (3 # 4)) = ?

A. -14

B. -8

C. 4

D. 8

E. 14

What symbolism means is that they will use a symbol to represent a math function. In this case when you see the #, it means that you do 3 times the first number – 2 times the second number. And just like "normal" math problems, you need to start with the parentheses first. 3(3) – 2(4) = 9 – 8 = 1

Now you plug 2 # 1 into the equations. 3(2)-2(1) = 4 Choice C is correct!

Binomials & Quadratics

To find the roots of a polynomial, all you have to do is figure out what values of x will give you 0 for y (in other words, what the x-intercepts are). There are a three ways that you have to determine what the **roots** are.

1. The easiest way is to **factor** the problem, and then set each "term" equal to zero.

    x² – 2x + 1 = _____ =

2. Another way to determine the roots is to use the **quadratic formula**: $\dfrac{-b \pm \sqrt{b^2 - 4ac}}{2a}$. You use this when you have an equation that is in the form $ax^2 + bx + c = 0$ that you can't factor. The two answers that you get are called roots.

    Why will you have two answers? Because the x is squared!

3. If you aren't a fan of the quadratic formula or factoring, you can always use your calculator to **graph** the equation. The roots will be where the graph crosses the x-axis.

    Example 23: Which of the following is a solution of the expression $3x^2 + x - 4$?

    A. -3

    B. $-\dfrac{4}{3}$

    C. -1

    D. 0

    E. $\dfrac{4}{3}$

    So let's pretend that I don't know how to solve this problem using Algebra, so I'm going to "plug" in the answer choices! A solution means that when I plug in the number, I will get zero as an answer. I'm going to start in the middle with -1, $3(-1)^2 + (-1) - 4 = 3 - 1 - 4 \neq 0$. The next easiest number to try is

0, $3(0)^2 + (0) - 4 = -4 \neq 0$. Now let's try $\frac{4}{3}$, $3(\frac{4}{3})^2 + (\frac{4}{3}) - 4 = = \frac{16}{3} + \frac{4}{3} - 4 \neq 0$

Boy, this sure isn't a lot of fun with all these fractions! Now let's try $\frac{-4}{3}$,

$3(-\frac{4}{3})^2 + (-\frac{4}{3}) - 4 = 0$! Yeah!! After all that work, the answer is B!

Practice Problems:

Red Book Test 2	Red Book Test 3	Red Book Test 4	Red Book Test 5
22, 28	23, 31, 47, 58	7, 55	None

Radical Expressions

There will be some questions that will have square roots in the answer choices (e.g. $\sqrt{3}$). If you solve the problem and get a decimal, you still might have the right answer; it is just in a different form. Type all of the answer choices into your calculator to see which one matches your decimal!

If you want to figure out how to get the answer without using your calculator, chances are that you have to simplify the radical.

To do this, break the number under the radical into its prime factors.
$\sqrt{50} = \sqrt{2 \cdot 5 \cdot 5}$

Next, pull out groups of the same number. If you are taking the square root, you need two of the same number to pull it out. If you are taking the cube root, you need 3, etc.
$\sqrt{50} = \sqrt{2 \cdot 5 \cdot 5} = 5\sqrt{2}$

What you can't pull out has to stay under the radical.

Example 21. If x is a real number such that $x^4 = 81$, then $x^2 - x$?

    A. 0
    B. 3
    C. 6
    D. 9
    E. 81

To solve this problem, I need to figure out what x is! You can either take the fourth root of 81, or you can try plugging in some numbers. $2^4=16$ $3^4=81$ So x has to be 3! Now I just need to plug it into the problem they give me, $3^2 - 3 = 9 - 3 = 6$ The answer is C.

Example 22. In the equation $x^2 + mx + n$, m and n are integers. The *only* possible value for x is –3. What is the value of m?

F.   3

G.   -3

H.   6

J.   -6

K.   9

This is the type of problem that would appear in the last 20 questions on the math test because you definitely have to have an understanding of the math concept of factoring to even grasp what the question is asking. If the *only* possible value for x is -3, then that means that I have only one term, but it has to be squared. $(x+3)^2 = 0 = (x+3)(x+3) = x^2 + 6x + 9$. This means that $m=6$, which is choice H.

Practice Problems:

Red Book Test 2	Red Book Test 3	Red Book Test 4	Red Book Test 5
40, 49	27	35	41

Inequalities

To solve inequalities, treat the < or > sign like it is an equal sign. You want to get x on one side of the sign, and everything else on the other. The only difference between inequalities and equations is that if you multiply or divide by a negative number, you have to flip the sign.

The only difference between inequalities and equations is that if you multiply or divide by a negative number, you have to flip the signs.

Example 23. If x and y are real number such that $x > 1$ and $y < -1$, then which of the following inequalities *must* be true?

A. $\dfrac{x}{y} > 1$

B. $|x|^2 > |y|$

C. $\dfrac{x}{3} - 5 > \dfrac{y}{3} - 5$

D. $x^2 + 1 > y^2 + 1$

E. $x^{-2} > y^{-2}$

The easiest way to solve this problem is to pick some numbers for x and y; we just need to make sure that we follow the directions they gave us in the question stem. Let's pick $x=2$ because x needs to be greater than 1. Let's pick $y=-6$ because y needs to be smaller than -1.

A. $\dfrac{2}{-3} > 1$ This is NOT true

B. $|2|^2 > |-6|$ 4 is not greater than 6, so this is NOT true.

C. $\dfrac{2}{3} - 5 > \dfrac{-6}{3} - 5$ This IS true! (check it in your calculator!)

D. $2^2 + 1 > (-6)^2 + 1$ This is NOT true.

E. $2^{-2} > (-6)^{-2}$ This is true with these numbers, but it we plugged in $x=6$ and $y=-2$, it would NOT be true.

Example 24. What are the real values of x that satisfy $-(x-1) > -x(x+1)$?

F. All real x

G. No real x

H. $x > 1$

J. $-1 < x < 1$

K. $x > 1$ or $x < -1$

You can plug in numbers for this one by using your answer choices for guidance, but this one is easier to solve if you use your algebra skills.

$-(x-1) > -x(x+1) = -x+1 > -x^2 - x$ and now let's get all of the terms on the same side:

$x^2 + 1 > 0$ and since our x terms cancelled, this is an easier problem now!

$x^2 > -1$... and guess what!??! This will ALWAYS be true, because whenever you square a number, it will be positive! So the answer is F!

Practice Problems:

Red Book Test 2	Red Book Test 3	Red Book Test 4	Red Book Test 5
26, 27	32	19, 56	11, 48, 53

Absolute Value Equations

Absolute value is the distance from zero, which is why it can never be a negative number. You treat the absolute value like parentheses – whatever is inside needs to be done first. Then you take the positive of any number that you get.

$$|-3+1| = |-2| = 2$$

The easiest way to solve absolute value equations is to plug in numbers!

To solve algebraically, you get the absolute value on one side, and everything else on the other. Then you set up two equations:

$|x-1| = 7$ becomes $x-1 = 7$ and $x-1 = -7$

So, $x = 8$ or $x = -6$

Some of the hardest problems on the ACT might combine inequalities and absolute values. You still use the same concept of setting up two inequalities, but now one will be the same sign and the other will be the opposite sign: both the inequality sign and positive/negative sign.

$|x-1| > 7$ becomes $x-1 > 7$ or $x-1 < -7$

So, $x > 8$ or $x < -6$

Absolute value bars are like special parentheses. You do what is inside the bars first, but only positive numbers come out!

Example 25. What are the real solutions to the equation $|x|^2 + 2|x| - 3 = 0$?

    A. ± 1
    B. ± 3
    C.   1 and 3
    D.   -1 and -3
    E. ± 1 and ± 3

You can totally plug in your answer choices on this one! Both 1 and -1 work when I plug them in 1+2-3=0, 3 and -3 don't work (9+6-3 does not equal 0) so the correct answer is A!

Practice Problems:

Red Book Test 2	Red Book Test 3	Red Book Test 4	Red Book Test 5
8, 49	None	10	4, 53

Systems of Equations

A solution to a system of equations is the one point where the two lines meet! There are three ways to solve systems of equations.

1. Substitution – you solve for one variable and substitute it into the other equation

   $3x - 4 = t$ and $3t + x = 0$

   I can plug the first equation into the second equation to solve for x.

   $3(2x - 4) + x = 0$

   $6x - 12 + x = 0$

   $7x - 12 = 0$

   $7x = 12$

   $x = \dfrac{12}{7}$ and then I plug this into the first equation to find the value of t.

   $3(\dfrac{12}{7}) - 4 = \dfrac{36}{7} - \dfrac{28}{7} = \dfrac{8}{7} = t$

2. Combination – you add or subtract entire equations to get a variable to cancel

   $-x + y = 9$
   $\underline{2x - y = 2}$ when I add these two equations, the y's will cancel!
   $x = 11$

   And now I can plug the value of x into either equation to get the value of y.

   $-11 + y = 9$

   $y = 20$

3. Graphing – put the equations into $y = mx + b$ form, graph, and find where they intersect.

One of the three ways will usually be faster than the other two ways, but you will always get the same answer using any of the approaches.

Example 26. What is the x coordinate where the following two linear equations intersect?

$$2x + 2y = -3$$
$$-4x - 2y = 1$$

F. -2
G. -1
H. 0
J. 1
K. 2

Like I already mentioned, I can solve this any of the three ways listed above, but one of the ways is usually going to be faster. In this case, since the "y"s will cancel so nicely, it will be fastest to use elimination. You can also solve this problem by "plugging" in the answer choices for x!! If you "plug" you answer choices in, you will need to find the value of x that will give you the same value of y for both equations. I'm going to use elimination to solve this problem.

If I add the equations, I get $2x = -2$, which means $x = -1$ (choice J) is the correct answer.

Practice Problems:

Red Book Test 2	Red Book Test 3	Red Book Test 4	Red Book Test 5
18	39	15, 22	13

Sequences and Series

There are two types of sequences and series that appear on the ACT: arithmetic and geometric. A couple of vocabulary words that are important in these problems are "finite" and "infinite". **Finite** means that there are a limited number of terms. **Infinite** means that there is no end to the number of terms.

Arithmetic sequences are sequences where you add or subtract to get the next numbers.

What is the next term in the following sequences?

3, 6, 9, _____ (you add 3)   17, 11, 5, _____ (you subtract 6)

If I was asked to find the sum of the 17, 11, 5, -1 sequence above, I could easily add them into my calculator. This would take a little longer if I wanted to find the sum of all the numbers between 1 and 1000! In the first case, I get 32; in the second case, I will use the following formula.

$$S_n = \frac{n(a_1 + a_n)}{2}$$

This looks like a complicated formula, but let me explain what everything means. S_n means the sum of the terms. n is the number of terms. a_1 is the first term, and a_n is the last term. So for the sum of all the numbers between 1 and 1000, the formula would look like this:

$$S_n = \frac{1000(1 + 1000)}{2} = \frac{1000(1001)}{2} = 500{,}500$$

Another question regarding arithmetic sequences might deal with trying to find a certain term in the sequence. Again, referring to the sequences above, when I am trying to find the next term in the sequence 3, 6, 9, I can easily figure out that it is 12. If someone asked me to find the 30th term in the sequence, it would be harder to figure… unless I knew the equation!

$$a_n = a_1 + d(n - 1)$$

a_n is the term that we are looking for. a_1 is the first term. d is the difference between the terms (+ if I am adding and – if I'm subtracting), and n is the number of terms. If I'm trying to find the 30th term of the sequence 3, 6, 9:

$$a_{30} = 3 + 3(30 - 1) = 3 + 3(29) = 90$$

Geometric sequences are sequences where you multiply or divide to get the next numbers.

What is the next term in the following sequences?

4, 12, 36, _____ (you multiply by 3)   20, 10, 5, _____ (you divide by 2)

Practice Problems:

Red Book Test 2	Red Book Test 3	Red Book Test 4	Red Book Test 5
53	None	8	52

Functions (7-9 questions)

A function is a problem that can be written as f(x). This can be a little intimidating. f(x) is the same as saying "y" if it is easier to think about the problem that way. If there is anything in the parentheses other than "x", all you have to do is plug whatever is in the ( ) in for x! It will help you get the right answer if you keep whatever you plug in for x in ( ) when you put it in the problem.

Example 27. A function P is defined as follows:

for x > 0, $P(x) = x^5 + x^4 - 36x - 36$

for x < 0, $P(x) = -x^5 + x^4 + 36x - 36$

What is the value of P(-1)?

A. -70

B. -36

C. 0

D. 36

E. 70

The problem tells us exactly what to do! Remember, whatever is in the parentheses is what x is equal to, so x = -1 for the problem. Since x = -1, we plug it in the second equation: $P(x) = -x^5 + x^4 + 36x - 36$

$P(-1) = -(-1)^5 + (-1)^4 + 36(-1) - 36 = -(-1) + 1 - 36 - 36 = 70$ Choice E!

Practice Problems:

Red Book Test 2	Red Book Test 3	Red Book Test 4	Red Book Test 5
2, 19, 23, 25, 54	11	21, 50, 54	10, 31

Number Lines

Number line problems are easiest to solve if you draw a number line (shocking, isn't it!?)

Example 28. Points A, B, C, and D are on a line such that B is between A and C, and C is between B and D. The distance from A to B is 6 units. The distance from B to C is twice the distance from A to B, and the distance from C to D is twice the distance from B to C. What is the distance, in units, from the midpoint of BC to the midpoint of CD?

F. 18
G. 14
H. 12
J. 9
K. 6

It is almost like reading a different language until you a draw a picture, and then everything starts to fall into place.

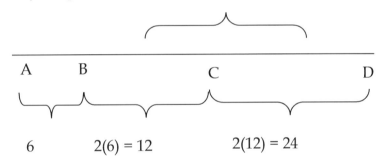

6   2(6) = 12   2(12) = 24

From the midpoint of BC to the midpoint of CD would be 6 + 12 = 18. F!

Practice Problems:

Red Book Test 2	Red Book Test 3	Red Book Test 4	Red Book Test 5
11	None	12	47

Domain and Range

Domain and range have to do with graphing. Asking about the domain is the same as asking what the x values of a graph are, and asking about the range is like asking about the y values. If you get confused, try to remember that they are in alphabetical order – **d**omain with **x** and **r**ange with **y**.

There are a couple things to keep in mind about domain. When you are graphing a function that has a fraction in it, the denominator of the fraction can never equal 0. Have a fraction with a zero in the denominator is like swearing in math – you don't want to do it!

$$y = \frac{x+3}{x-1}$$

In this problem, $x-1$ CANNOT equal 0, so this means that the domain of the problem is $x \neq 1$

Another thing to keep in mind with domain is that if there is a square root in the problem, whatever is under the square root has to be greater than or equal to zero.

$$y = \sqrt{x+4}$$

In this problem $x+4 \geq 0$, which means the domain would be $x \geq -4$

Practice Problems:

Red Book Test 2	Red Book Test 3	Red Book Test 4	Red Book Test 5
None	None	20, 50	37

Transformations

Translations and transformations mean moving graphs around on the x-y coordinate plane. There are five simple rules you need to follow for transformation questions.

Rule 1: The number on the outside of the parentheses moves the graph up or down (same)
Rule 2: The number on the inside of the parentheses moves the graph to the left or right (opposite)
Rule 3: The number in front of the x stretches the graph up or down (same)
Rule 4: The number in front of the variable in the parentheses stretches the

graph left or right (opposite)
Rule 5: Negative signs flip the graph over an axis.

If I am going to try graphing the following problem:

$y = (x+1)^2 - 4$, I would be using the shape of an x^2 graph (a parabola). According to Rule 1, the number outside the parentheses moves the graph up and down. So the -4 will move the graph down 4, because outside the parentheses behaves exactly like you would expect it to. According to Rule 2, I will also move the graph to the left 1because inside the parentheses moves the graph left and right, and it moves the direction that is opposite of what I would expect it to. Even through it is a +1, it moves to the left one.

Practice Problems:

Red Book Test 2	Red Book Test 3	Red Book Test 4	Red Book Test 5
None	None	32	45

Slope

$y = mx + b$ is a very common concept that is tested on the ACT. Remember, "m" is the slope, and "b" is the y-intercept (where the line crosses the y-axis). For two points, (x_1, y_1) and (x_2, y_2), you can find the slope with the following equation:

$$m = \frac{rise}{run} = \frac{y_2 - y_1}{x_x - x_1}$$

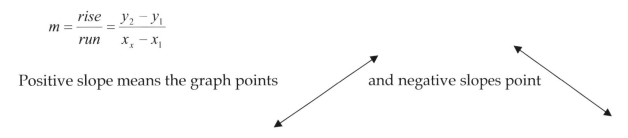

Positive slope means the graph points   and negative slopes point

For horizontal lines, ⟷ if this were a ski slope, you wouldn't go anywhere. The slope is 0.

For vertical lines,   if this were a ski slope… you would die! The slope is undefined.

Example 29. What is the slope of the line through (-5,2) and (6,7) in the standard (x,y) coordinate plane?

    A.   9

    B.   5

    C.   -5

    D. $\dfrac{5}{11}$

    E. $-\dfrac{5}{11}$

If you don't remember the formula, trying plotting the points on a graph and then count up and then over. If you don't even remember up and over, you would at least be able to tell whether the slope is positive or negative.

I'm going to use the formula:

$$m = \frac{7-2}{6-(-5)} = \frac{5}{11},$$ so the answer is D.

Example 30. The slope of the line with equation $y = ax + b$ is greater than the slope of the line with equation $y = cx + b$. Which of the following statements *must* be true about the relationship between a and c?

    F. $a \leq c$

    G. $a < c$

    H. $a = c$

    J. $a > c$

    K. $a \geq c + 1$

If we know that the slope of the equation with a is greater than the slope of the equation with c, then you already know the answer. J has to be the answer because $a > c$

Practice Problems:

Red Book Test 2	Red Book Test 3	Red Book Test 4	Red Book Test 5
25, 52	17, 26	31	12

Parallel and Perpendicular Lines

Parallel lines have the same slope.

Perpendicular lines have opposite reciprocal slopes.

What is the slope of a line parallel to y = -3x+4? Parallel lines have the same slope, so m = -3

What is the slope of a line perpendicular to y = -3x + 4? Perpendicular lines have opposite, reciprocal, so in this case, $m = \dfrac{1}{3}$

A lot of times, when we talk about parallel lines, we also talk about lines that have no solutions. There are three different types of lines that will appear on the test:

- Lines that never intersect (there is no solution) are parallel lines. Since they have the same slope, it means they will never meet.
- Lines that have an infinite number of solutions are the same line. They intersect along the entire line because they are the same!
- Lines that have one solution, which is actually most of the lines that you will see on the test. The lines will intersect at one point only, and that point is considered the solution.

Example 31. For what value of a would the following system of equations have an infinite number of solutions?

$$2x - y = 8$$
$$6x - 3y = 4a$$

A. 2

B. 6

C. 8

D. 24

E. 32

In order to have infinite solutions, they need to be the same line. From looking at the coefficient for the x, it appears that we need to multiply the first equation by 3 to get the second equation. So in order for the lines to be the same line, I need to multiply 8 by 3, which is 24. That means that $4a = 24$, so $a = 6$. B is the answer.

Red Book Test 2	Red Book Test 3	Red Book Test 4	Red Book Test 5
50	None	None	None

Geometry (7-9 questions)

Now let's talk some geometry! The awesome thing about geometry is that drawing pictures can help you a lot through these problems. And even though the instructions on the math portion of the test tell you that the figures are NOT drawn to scale, you can use the pictures they give you to help eliminate answer choices!

Use the pictures (or draw pictures) as much as possible on geometry problems to get to the right answer as quickly as possible!

Midpoints

The midpoint is one of formulas that you will need to know for the ACT, but if you can't remember the exact formula, there are two ways to get to the correct answer. You can try to remember that the midpoint is literally the middle point: you just take an average. If you can't remember either of those, try plotting the two points on a graph and using your answer choices.

$$mid = \left(\frac{x_2 - x_1}{2}, \frac{y_2 - y_1}{2} \right)$$

Example 32. The coordinates of the endpoints of $\overline{CD}$, in the standard (x, y) coordinate plane, are (-4,-2) and (14,2). What is the x-coordinate of the midpoint of $\overline{CD}$?

    F.   0

    G.   2

    H.   5

    J.   9

    K.   10

As I mentioned above, you can plot the points on a graph, think about it being the average of the x-values, or use the formula. midpoint

$$= \frac{-4+14}{2} = \frac{10}{2} = 5 \quad \text{Choice H.}$$

Practice Problems:

Red Book Test 2	Red Book Test 3	Red Book Test 4	Red Book Test 5
21	38	None	None

Distance

Another formula that you need to know is the distance formula, and this one might be harder for you to remember. If you don't remember the formula, I ALWAYS want you to plot the points to see if it can help you. For the distance formula, after you plot the points, you can turn them into a triangle. To find the distance, use the Pythagorean Theorem ($a^2 + b^2 = c^2$) to get the answer.

$$dist = \sqrt{(x_2 - x_1)^2 + (y_2 - y_1)^2}$$

Example 33. If we think of a map as an x-y coordinate plane, let's say that Chicago is at (0, 200) and Orlando is at (300, -200). What is the distance, in coordinate units, between these two cities?

    A. 200
    B. 300
    C. 400
    D. 500
    E. 600

As mentioned above, you can plot the points on a graph and use $a^2 + b^2 = c^2$ or you can use the distance formula $dist = \sqrt{(x_2 - x_1)^2 + (y_2 - y_1)^2}$

$$dist = \sqrt{(300 - 0)^2 + (-200 - 200)^2} = \sqrt{900 + 1600} = \sqrt{2500} = 500$$

Choice D. Although when you actually drive between these two cities, it feels like ∞.

Practice Problems:

Red Book Test 2	Red Book Test 3	Red Book Test 4	Red Book Test 5
17, 33	None	30	32, 58

Graphing – Points, Lines, Polynomials, Circles

The most common graphing question on the ACT is regarding lines. Anything that can be written in the form $Ax + By = C$ is a line and can be graphed on the x-y coordinate plane. If you are not sure what to do on a graphing question, or any question involving points on the coordinate plane, remember: when in doubt, plot it out!

If you aren't sure what to do for a graph problem, graph it on your calculator!

Some graphs that might appear on the ACT are below:

Line: $y = mx + b$

Parabola: anything with x^2 or y^2

Circle: $(x - h)^2 + (y - k)^2 = r^2$ where the center is (h, k) and the radius is r

Polynomial: $(x - h)(x - k)(x + m) = y$ where $(x - h)$ is called a factor

You will have one circle equation. Remember 2 things to get it right:

-Remember that the center is at the opposite: (-1,1) will appear as 1 and -1 in the equation

-Remember that the equation will equal the radius squared.

Example 34. Which of the following describes the graph $(x+2)^2 + (y-2)^2 = 9$?

    F.   A line that goes through the point (-2, 2)

    G.   A parabola with the vertex at (-2, 2)

    H.   An ellipse centered at (-2, 2)

    J.   A circle with a radius of 9

    K.   A circle with a radius of 3

Both x and y are squared, so it isn't a line or parabola. It is the equation for a circle. Check out Tutor Tina above for the hints… opposite signs and radius squared. K is the answer.

Example 35. What are the quadrants of the standard (x, y) coordinate plane below that contain points on the graph of the equation $4x - 2y = 8$?

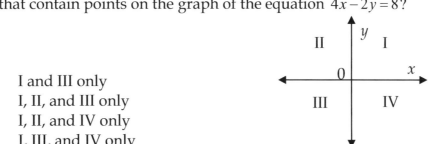

    A.   I and III only
    B.   I, II, and III only
    C.   I, II, and IV only
    D.   I, III, and IV only
    E.   II, III, and IV only

You can graph this on your calculator, but you need to put the equation in slope-intercept form first, $y = mx + b$ so you need to solve for y. $y = 2x - 4$

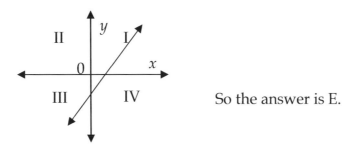

So the answer is E.

Practice Problems:

Red Book Test 2	Red Book Test 3	Red Book Test 4	Red Book Test 5
16, 32	17, 59	8, 20, 32, 54, 56, 59	2, 9, 45, 60

Angles and Lines

The above angles are supplementary. They add up to 180º.

Complimentary angels add up to 90º. If you get confused between supplementary and complimentary, remember that compliments make you feel all **right** (as in a right angle)! (I know, bad joke, but maybe it will help you remember the difference between them!)

Below is a picture of parallel lines, and the line that cuts across them is called a transversal (you don't need to know that word for the test.) When a transversal cuts across parallel lines, you get some special relationships!

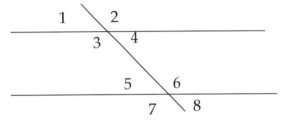

If $\angle 1$ is $23°$, what are the measurements of the remaining angles on the figure?

$$\angle 1 = \angle 4 = \angle 5 = \angle 8 = 23°$$

$$\angle 2 = \angle 3 = \angle 6 = \angle 7 = 180° - 23° = 157°$$

You can also think about it as all acute angles are equal, and all obtuse angles are equal.

Example 36. In the figure below, the line *l* is parallel to line *m*. Transversals *t* and *u* intersect as point *A* on *l* and intersect at *m* at points *C* and *B* respectively. Point *X* is on *m*, the measure of ∠*ACX* is 130°, and the measure of ∠*BAC* is 80°. How many of the angles formed by rays of *l, m, t,* and *u* have measure 50°?

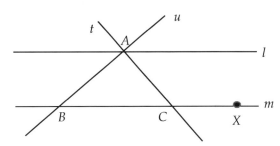

F.   4

G.   6

H.   8

J.   10

K.   12

On any geometry problem, you want to start off by marking up the figure with the information we are given in the question.

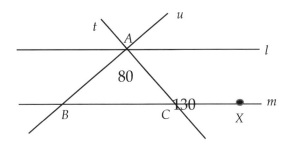

Now we add information based on what we know from geometry – supplementary angles, vertical angels, and using the parallel lines. It is important to mark up all of the angles in order to make sure we get the count correct.

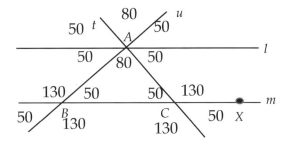

Count up all the 50° angles, and we have 8 of them – answer H!

Practice Problems:

Red Book Test 2	Red Book Test 3	Red Book Test 4	Red Book Test 5
6, 43	10, 44	6, 36, 44, 46	19, 51

Triangles

The most common shapes that appear on the ACT are triangles.

How many degrees are in a triangle? **180°**

How do you find the area of a triangle? $\frac{1}{2}bh$

And the most common triangles on the test are right triangles. (right triangles have a 90° angle)

When you have a right triangle, and you know the length of two sides, you can figure out the third side using a formula known as Pythagorean Theorem. The a and b sides are known as the legs, and the c side is always across from the right angle (known as the hypotenuse).

$$a^2 + b^2 = c^2$$

There are some special right triangles that appear frequently on the test. When you can use the Pythagorean Theorem with integers, those integers are called triplets. The good news is that if you recognize the triplets, you can save some time on the test. The even better news is that if you don't recognize the triplets, you can always use Pythagorean Theorem.

Triplets: 3, 4, 5 (or it might be multiplied by two 6, 8, 10) and 5, 12, 13

Some other special triangles are $45° - 45° - 90°$ and $30° - 60° - 90°$ triangles. There are some special ratios between the sides of these triangles that will always be true. If you don't remember the ratios, you can use trigonometry.

$45° - 45° - 90°$

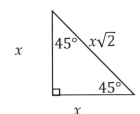

$30° - 60° - 90°$

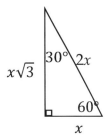

Here are some hints on how to remember the ratios above:

$45° - 45° - 90°$: Two angles are the same, and so the $\sqrt{2}$ goes with this triangle

$30° - 60° - 90°$: The x goes across from the smallest angle, 2 times 30 is 60, so the $2x$ goes on the side that is between those two angles, and $\sqrt{3}$ goes with this triangle because 30, 60, and 90 are all related to 3. I realize that they are also all related to 2, but this is just how I remember it!

Example 37. What is the length, in feet, of the hypotenuse of a right triangle with legs that are 6 feet long and 7 feet long, respectively?

A. $\sqrt{13}$
B. $\sqrt{85}$
C. 13
D. 21
E. 42

When you don't have a picture for a geometry problem – make one!

6   And now we get to use the ever famous $a^2 + b^2 = c^2$

7

$$6^2 + 7^2 = 36 + 49 = 85 = c^2 \quad c = \sqrt{85} \text{ which is answer B.}$$

Practice Problems:

Red Book Test 2	Red Book Test 3	Red Book Test 4	Red Book Test 5
10, 50, 52	10, 20, 28, 44, 45, 56	6, 13, 18, 28, 44, 48	16, 32, 33, 35

Circles

Any problem involving a circle will involve finding or using the radius to solve the problem.

The radius is half of the diameter.

There are **360°** in a circle.

Area of a circle = $\boldsymbol{\pi r^2}$

Circumference of a circle (distance around the outside) = $\boldsymbol{2\pi r}$

It is pretty rare for the test to ask you about the area of a sector or length of an arc, but if it does have a questions regarding these, you will not be given the formulas. However, there is a very easy way to remember these formulas. A sector is related the area of the entire circle; in fact, it is a fraction of the area of the circle. That fraction is the degree of the angle out of the total number of degrees in a circle. The same is true for the length of an arc, but it is related to circumference instead of area.

Area of a sector = $\dfrac{\boldsymbol{x}}{\boldsymbol{360}}\boldsymbol{\pi r^2}$

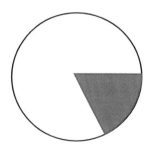

Length of an arc $= \frac{x}{360} 2\pi r$

Example 38. If the circumference of a circle is 10π, what is the area of the circle?

        F. 5π
        G. 10π
        H. 25π
        J. 100π
        K. 400π

Like I mentioned earlier, to solve circle problems, you need to figure out the radius. If the circumference is $10\pi = 2\pi r$, then $r = 5$. Now we can use the area formula, $A = \pi r^2 = \pi 5^2 = 25\pi$. The answer is H.

Practice Problems:

Red Book Test 2	Red Book Test 3	Red Book Test 4	Red Book Test 5
10, 30	18, 29, 34	36, 52	7, 23, 58

Quadrilaterals (and Polygons)

Some quadrilateral facts:

A quadrilateral has 4 sides, and **360°**.

To find the number of degrees in a polygon,

Start with a triangle: 3 sides is $180°$
Then for every side you add to the figure, you add $180°$ (you are literally adding a $180°$ line).

There is a formula that you can memorize, but for the frequency of questions about the interior degrees of a shape appears on the ACT, it isn't worth your time or effort to memorize!

In case you want to know it – the number of degrees in a polygon of n sides is:

$$Degrees = 180(n-2)$$

Pentagon:

      How many sides?   5   How many degrees?   **540°**

Hexagon:

      How many sides?   6   How many degrees?   720°

Heptagon:

      How many sides?   7   How many degrees?   900°

Octagon:

      How many sides?   8   How many degrees?   1080°

A question that appears on the test rarely regards the diagonals of a polygon. I can give you the formula to determine the number of diagonals in a polygon (and I will), but it is easier if you draw a picture and count the diagonals.

How many diagonals are there in a hexagon?

I can draw 3 diagonals from one vertex, and I have 6 vertices. I would have 18 diagonals, but then I would be counting every diagonal twice. So I have to divide by 2 = 9!

$$number\ of\ diagonals = \frac{(number\ of\ sides)(number\ of\ sides-3)}{2}$$

Practice Problems:

Red Book Test 2	Red Book Test 3	Red Book Test 4	Red Book Test 5
6, 38, 51	18, 24, 25, 36	1, 24, 25, 29, 30	7, 8, 9, 26, 27, 36, 38, 57

Area

The area of a square is s^2 (side squared).

The area of a rectangle is $A = bh$ (base times height).

The area of a parallelogram is actually the same formula, $\underline{A = bh}$ (base times height). The only difference is that the height is the vertical distance, not the side length. If you have a hard time visualizing this, think about cutting off a triangle on one side of the parallelogram and moving it to the other side.

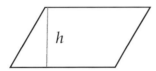

The area of a trapezoid is $A = \frac{b_1 + b_2}{2} h$.

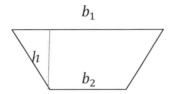

If you don't want to memorize the area of a trapezoid formula, think about breaking the trapezoid into two triangles and a rectangle.

Example 39. The length of a rectangle is 3 times the length of a smaller rectangle. The 2 rectangles have the same width. The area of the smaller rectangle is A square units. The area of the larger rectangle is kA square units. Which of the following is the value of k?

    A. $\dfrac{1}{9}$

    B. $\dfrac{1}{3}$

    C.   1

    D.   3

    E.   9

Again, a geometry problem without pictures – make them!!!

$$Area = A$$

$$Area = ka$$

If you still aren't sure how to approach the problem, let's try "plugging" in some numbers. Let's say that the length is 3 and the height is 2.

3

2 $Area = ka = 2(3) = 6$

The length of the second rectangle is 3 times larger than the first, and it is the same height.

$$3(3) = 9$$

2 $Area = ka = 2(9) = 18$

Now I need to compare the area of the two rectangles. I know that:
Area of the first rectangle is 6 and that the area of the second rectangle is 18, therefore it is 3 times as large! $k = 3$. Answer D!

Example 40. Each side of the smaller square in the figure below is x inches long, and each side of the larger square is c inches longer than a side of the smaller square. The area of the larger square is how many square inches greater than the area of the smaller square?

F. c^2

G. xc

H. $4c$

J. $(x+c)^2$

K. $2xc+c^2$

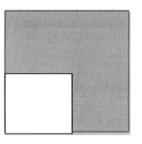

This looks like an incredibly difficult problem, but when you "plug" in some numbers, it is SO much easier! Let's say that $x = 2$ and $c = 3$. Then the area of the large square is $(2 + 3)(2 + 3) = (5)(5) = 25$, and the area of the smaller square is $(2)(2) = 4$. To get the area of the shaded region, I subtract the area of the smaller square from the area of the larger square $= 25 - 4 = 21$. Now all I need to do is plug $x = 2$ and $c = 3$ into the answer choices to see which answer choice gives me 21 as the answer!

F. $3^2 = 9$

G. $(2)(3) = 6$

H. $4(3) = 12$

J. $(2+3)^2 = 25$

K. $2(2)(3) + 3^2 = 12 + 9 = 21$ This matches what we got; it's the correct answer!

Practice Problems:

Red Book Test 2	Red Book Test 3	Red Book Test 4	Red Book Test 5
13, 30, 34, 38	14, 18, 24, 25, 29, 51	1, 18, 25, 29	8, 23, 24, 26, 36, 38, 57

Perimeter

Think of perimeter as walking around the outside of a shape. You figure out what each side should be and then add them all up! If you are having a difficult time guessing at what side lengths should be, then think about it as taking a step back from the picture to see the 'bigger" picture. (See Example 41)

Example 41. In the 8-sided figure below, adjacent sides meet at right angles and the lengths given are in meters. What is the perimeter of the figure, in meters?

A.   40
B.   80
C.   120
D.   160
E.   400

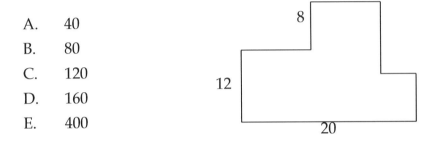

We actually only know lengths for 3 sides of the figure, but that is all we need to solve this problem if you look at the bigger picture. If the 2 left sides (12 and 8) add up to be 20, what do you think the two right sides need to add up to be? That is right: 20! Now we know the bottom is a total of 20 long, so what do the top three lines need to add up to? 20! Now we know the overall total length of each side, so we just need to add all those up. $20 + 20 + 20 + 20 = 80$ Answer B.

Practice Problems:

Red Book Test 2	Red Book Test 3	Red Book Test 4	Red Book Test 5
7, 51	14, 28	24	7, 27, 57

Visualizations

You will not actually be asked to do a proof on the ACT, but the concepts that you have learned about while doing proofs will be tested. Being able to visualize moving a shape around – flipping it or rotating it – will help you solve these problems! Remember that moving a shape around will not affect the size, area, angles, or side lengths!

Example 42. If the two triangles below are congruent, then their sides are proportional. The trick for working through problems involving proportions is to keep the sides you are comparing and the shapes that you are comparing in the correct places in the ratios. For the triangles in the figure below, which of the following ratios of side lengths is equivalent to the ratio of the perimeter of $\triangle ABC$ to the perimeter of $\triangle DAB$?

F. $AB : AD$

G. $AB : BD$

H. $AD : BD$

J. $BC : AD$

K. $BC : BD$

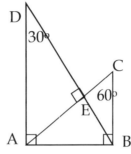

The easiest way to solve this problem is to flip the triangles around so that they match up for the angles.

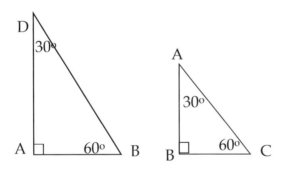

When I flip the triangles around, and then look through the answer choices, it is only answer choice A that matches sides on both triangles.

Volume

Area is for 2-dimensional shapes, and volume is for 3-dimensional shapes.

You will have to know how to find the volume of a cube, a rectangular prism, and a cylinder on the ACT. To get the formula, think about the 2-D shape that is the bottom of the 3-D shape. You find the area of the 2-D shape, and then multiply it by how many of the shapes are "stacked" on top of one another – the height!

$$V_{cube} = s^3$$

$$V_{rect\_prism} = lwh$$

$$V_{cylinder} = \pi r^2 h$$

Cubes, cylinders, and rectangular prisms are just a few of the words that are used to describe 3-dimensional shapes. These will be some of the most difficult Plane Geometry questions on the test; so if you have a hard time with visualizing in 3-D, don't worry too much. There will only be 1 or 2 questions on the whole test!

To solve these problems, try to picture what the problem is describing and go from there!

Example 43. Josh has installed a swimming pool on level ground. The pool is a right cylinder with a diameter of 24 feet and a height of 6 feet. To the nearest cubic foot, what is the volume of water that will be in the pool when it is filled with water to a depth of 5 feet?

A. 942
B. 1,885
C. 2,262
D. 9,047
E. 11,310

You can probably guess the first thing I'm going to tell you to do. If you can't guess it, you haven't been reading through the explanations for the other geometry problems… draw a picture!

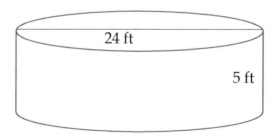

Again, finding the radius to very important. We are given the diameter in the problem, so we need to divide that in half to get the radius. $r = 12$

$Volume = \pi r^2 h = \pi 12^2 (5) = 720\pi \approx 2,261$ Choice C is the right answer!

Practice Problems:

Red Book Test 2	Red Book Test 3	Red Book Test 4	Red Book Test 5
14	42, 43	5, 43	59

Surface Area

Both volume and surface area are for 3-dimensional objects, but whereas volume is about the "inside" of the object, surface area is all about the outside! Surface area is literally taking area to the next level.

To find the surface area of an object, you find the area of each side of the object and then add them all up!

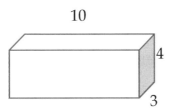

Area of the top = (10)(3) = 30
Area of the bottom = (10)(3) = 30
Area of the left side = (4)(3) = 12
Area of the right side = (4)(3) = 12
Area of the front side = (10)(4) = 40
Area of the back side = (10)(4) = 40

Now add up all the areas:

30+30+12+12+40+40 = 164

Trigonometry

You will be able to solve 2 of the 4 trig problems on the ACT using SOHCAHTOA. Always look from the direction of the angle the question is asking about to label the sides.

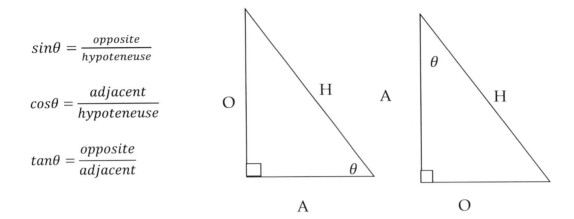

$$sin\theta = \frac{opposite}{hypoteneuse}$$

$$cos\theta = \frac{adjacent}{hypoteneuse}$$

$$tan\theta = \frac{opposite}{adjacent}$$

If you are given a trig problem without a diagram, draw a triangle, pick an angle, and label your sides accordingly.

Example 44. Kayleigh is working on assembling a pool that is 6 feet tall. The directions for assembling the pool state that the ladder should be placed at an angle of $75°$ relative to level ground. Which of the following expressions involving tangent gives the distance, in feet, that the bottom of the ladder should be placed away from the bottom edge of the pool in order to comply with the directions?

F. $\dfrac{6}{\tan 75°}$

G. $\dfrac{\tan 75°}{6}$

H. $\dfrac{1}{6\tan 75°}$

J. $6\tan 75°$

K. $\tan(6 \cdot 75)°$

We need to start off by drawing a picture and labeling what we know (shocked, aren't you!?!?)

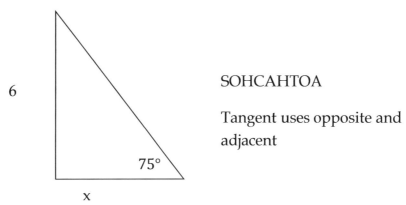

SOHCAHTOA

Tangent uses opposite and adjacent

$\tan 75° = \frac{6}{x}$ and solving for x gives us: $x = \frac{6}{\tan 75°}$ Choice F is the answer.

Practice Problems:

Red Book Test 2	Red Book Test 3	Red Book Test 4	Red Book Test 5
20, 48	37	44	16, 30

Values and Properties of Trigonometric Functions

To find the value of an angle (sometimes referred to as θ), you need to use the inverse of the trig functions. To do this on your calculator, you need to hit the second button and then the trig function you want to use.

$$\sin \theta = \frac{1}{2} \qquad \theta = 30° \qquad \cos^{-1} \frac{-\sqrt{3}}{2} = 150°$$

The reciprocal trig functions are different than the inverse trig functions. Remember when we talked way earlier in the math section about reciprocals flipping a fraction over? The same thing happens with trig functions:

$$\frac{1}{\sin} = \csc$$

$$\frac{1}{\cos} = \sec$$

$$\frac{1}{\tan} = \cot$$

How to remember which ones are paired together?

- Tangent and cotangent are easy to remember - the only ones with "t"
- Cosine pairs with secant - <u>cos</u> goes with <u>sec</u>
- Sine and cosecant are the only two left!

There are also questions on the exam that might deal with some harder trig concepts like law of cosines. You don't need to know the formulas though because they will be provided!

Red Book Test 2	Red Book Test 3	Red Book Test 4	Red Book Test 5
35	40, 50	42	49

Graphing Trigonometric Functions

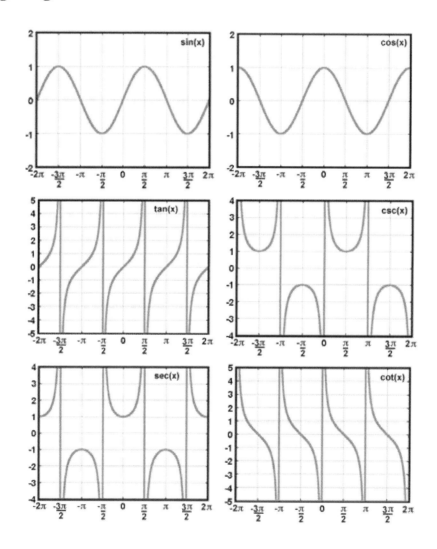

$y = a\sin(bx + c) + d$

a = amplitude – how high the graph goes

b = change in the period

c = phase shift (moves the graph left or right)

d = vertical shift (moves the graph up or down)

Even though there is this complicated looking equation, the two most common questions about a trig graph have to deal with amplitude and the period.

The amplitude is how far the graph moves from the middle line. You can take the highest y-value and subtract the lowest y-value, and then divide it by 2!

The period is how long it takes the graph to complete one cycle. That means that the graph will go up and then go down (or down and then up), but you are looking for how long it takes to COMPLETE a cycle.

Some of the hardest problems on the ACT **might** test the trig identities. The most common trig identity is: $\sin^2 \theta + \cos^2 \theta = 1$

Example 45. For x such that $0 < x < \dfrac{\pi}{2}$, the expression $sin^2x - 1 + cos^2x$ is equivalent to:

A.   0

B.   1

C.   2

D.   - tan x

E.   sin $2x$

Using the trig identity $\sin^2 \theta + \cos^2 \theta = 1$, I can substitute 1 into the equation for the $sin^2x + cos^2x$, which will give me $1 - 1 = 0$. A is the answer.

Practice Problems:

Red Book Test 2	Red Book Test 3	Red Book Test 4	Red Book Test 5
None	53	None	45

Conics

Parabolas, hyperbolas, ellipses, and circles all fall into the category of conics, but I have never seen a hyperbola on the test. These questions do not appear very often, so if you don't remember the formulas, it is no big deal! If you do remember, then it will be an easy problem!

Parabola: anything with x^2 or y^2

Circle: $(x-h)^2 + (y-k)^2 = r^2$ where the center is (h, k) and the radius is r

Hyperbola: $\frac{(x-h)^2}{a^2} - \frac{(y-k)^2}{b^2} = 1$ where the center is (h, k)

Ellipse: $\frac{(x-h)^2}{a^2} + \frac{(y-k)^2}{b^2} = 1$ where the center is (h, k)

Red Book Test 2	Red Book Test 3	Red Book Test 4	Red Book Test 5
None	None	52	58

Logic

There is a good chance that if you come across a logic problem (which only appears on maybe one out of every five tests) you will think, "Why is this on the math test? It doesn't feel like a math problem!" but it does fall under the category of geometry.

If, then

    If it is raining, then the sky is grey.

Inverse

    If it is not raining, then the sky is not grey.

Converse

If the sky is grey, then it is raining.

Contrapositive

If the sky in not grey, then it is not raining.

Practice Problems:

Red Book Test 2	Red Book Test 3	Red Book Test 4	Red Book Test 5
None	5	28	None

Statistics & Probability (5-7 questions)

Permutations & Combinations

Permutations and combinations are considered counting techniques. The most common question for permutations and combinations is easy to solve once you realize what you need to do!

Example 46: Dennis is at the Kingsley Sandwich Shop and has many choices for what to eat. There are 5 types of bread, 6 types of meat, and 3 types of soup. If Dennis chooses one type of bread, one type of meat, and one soup for lunch, how many different possibilities does Dennis have for lunch?

    F. 14
    G. 25
    H. 33
    J. 90
    K. 120

When you are only choosing one of each, all you need to remember to do on these types of problems is to multiply! (5)(6)(3) = 90. The answer is J

Sometimes there are questions involving the formulas for permutations and combinations. Permutations are for when order matters, and combinations are for when order doesn't matter. This is what the formulas look like:

$$_nP_r = \frac{n!}{(n-r)!}$$

$$_nC_r = \frac{n!}{r!\,(n-r)!}$$

The ! symbol is called a factorial (it doesn't mean that you just shout the letters). There is a button on your calculator for it located under the Math – Prob menu on the TI-83 or TI-84 calculators. What a factorial means is that you multiply that integer and all the integers below it. How it works is like this:

$$6! = (6)(5)(4)(3)(2)(1) = 720$$

At ACT High School, there are 10 people on the Improve Our Score Committee. How many possibilities are there for president and vice-president?

In this example, order matters, so I must use the Permutations formula (of the permutations button on my calculator.) I am choosing 2 people from 10 options.

$$_{10}P_2 = \frac{10!}{(10-2)!} = \frac{3628800}{40320} = 90$$

Practice Problems:

Red Book Test 2	Red Book Test 3	Red Book Test 4	Red Book Test 5
24, 55	8, 57	3, 51	44

Expected Value

Expected value has shown up on a couple of recent tests, so it is worth talking about. In an expected value problem, you are given a list of all possible values for a sample set and the probability of each of those values occurring. The expected value is a predicted value of a variable, calculated as the sum of all possible values each multiplied by the probability of its occurrence. Sounds like a bunch of math talk, so let me show you what I mean.

Example:

X	P(x)
0	0.850
1	0.120
2	0.015
3	0.010
4	0.005

To calculate expected value, you multiply the value (X) by the probability (P(x)) and then add them all together.

X	P(x)	X * p(x)
0	0.850	0
1	0.120	0.120
2	0.015	0.030
3	0.010	0.030
4	0.005	0.020
Sum		0.200

So the expected value of this example is 0.200

Practice Problems:

Red Book Test 2	Red Book Test 3	Red Book Test 4	Red Book Test 5
41	46	None	54

Data Collection Methods

In Statistics, there are several ways to collect data. This really is more of an exercise of knowing some vocabulary, and even if you can't remember what all of the data collection methods are, you can use process of elimination to hopefully eliminate some wrong answer choices. Now let's review some vocab!

Population: entire pool from which a sample is drawn (all seniors in a high school)

Sample: smaller representative group of a population (Math classes that contain only seniors)

Randomization: choosing without bias

Something is random if everything in the sample set has an equal chance of being chosen.

Example: Pulling different colored jelly beans out of a bag.

Experiment: The sample is split into a control group and an experimental group, where the only difference between the groups is that one is receiving a placebo (nothing is really done to the group) and then the group trying what is being tested.

Census: an official count or survey of a population

Observational study: observes individuals and measures variable of interest but does not attempt to influence the responses.

Sets

You know that you have a problem dealing with sets when the problem starts with giving you numbers related to categories. The easiest way to solve the problem is to draw a picture. I'll walk through an example to show you what I mean.

Example 47: At Wolverine High School (which just happens to be in Ann Arbor, Michigan), there are 28 students in an AP Calculus class, and there are 32 students in the AP Statistics class. If there are 40 students enrolled in these two AP math classes at Wolverine High School, how many students are taking both AP Calculus and AP Statistics this semester?

A. 20
B. 28
C. 32
J. 40
K. 60

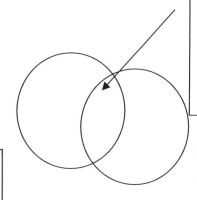

If we have 40 students total, we need to add up how many students are in the two classes (28+32) = 60. We only have 40 students, so 60 – 40 = 20. There must be 20 in BOTH

AP Calculus

28 students

AP Statistics

32 students

Practice Problems:

Red Book Test 2	Red Book Test 3	Red Book Test 4	Red Book Test 5
47	None	None	None

Residuals

A residual is the difference between an observed value and the value predicted by the regression line. In this case, you will be given a "regression line" equation, which is an equation that is a line of best fit for the data. In the real world, the data that we collect is never going to be perfect for an equation, but we can try to model the data with an equation. This equation is called the regression line when it is linear. Residuals are the difference between the value that we found in the real world and the value that we get if we use the equation.

Residual = (actual value) – (predicted value)

The best news is that if you don't understand this – no worries!! Look below to see how often it appears on tests!

Practice Problems:

Red Book Test 2	Red Book Test 3	Red Book Test 4	Red Book Test 5
None	59	None	None

READING

ANSWER THE QUESTION IN YOUR
OWN WORDS BEFORE LOOKING AT
THE ANSWER CHOICES

There are 4 passages on the reading test, and each passage has 10 questions.

You have 35 minutes total; this means you have approximately 8.5 minutes per passage.

The passages **always** appear in this order:

Prose Fiction

Social Studies

Humanities

Natural Sciences

One of the passages will have 2 smaller passages – Passage A and Passage B…. we'll talk strategy on this one in a little bit!

To get the most points, do your "easy" passages first.

What do I mean by that? Your "easy" passages are the passages that are the most interesting to you. Now don't get me wrong – almost all of the passages are INCREDIBLY boring. And I don't mean just a little boring… sometimes they are even painful to read! So if you are practicing and happen to find a type of passage that seems even a little bit more interesting to you than the other topics, that is definitely the passage type to begin with. For example, if you like science, then Natural Science might have the most interesting topics to you – you may want to work through the passages starting with Passage IV and ending with Passage I.

It also helps to know that questions appear in any order on the Reading test, and are not necessarily in order by difficulty or where the answers appear in the passage. This is helpful to know because if (or I should say WHEN) you come across a difficult question, you can skip it and try the other questions in the passage first. In fact, those 10 questions are all about the same passage, so a lot of times, one question might help you with an answer to another question.

> ### Game Plan for Reading
>
> 1. Read passage and annotate 1-2 words for each paragraph.
>
> 2. Read the question and predict your answer.
>
> 3. Pick the answer that best matches your prediction.

Game Plan for Reading

1. Read passage and annotate (only a couple words for each paragraph!)

Why read the passage first instead of looking through the questions and then reading?

> Now this goes against what an expert in **reading** might tell you. I have heard all different types of strategies: read the questions first, read the first sentence of every paragraph, read the first paragraph and the last paragraph only, etc. The list goes on and on. Now let me explain why the **TEST** expert feels reading the passage first is the best way to approach the test. You only have 8.5 minutes to 11 minutes to read the passage and answer all 10 questions. That is not a lot of time! So if you read the questions first, or read only part of the passage, you are going to end up RE-reading a lot during that 8.5 minutes! It is hard to have enough time to read the passage once and answer the questions. You definitely don't have a lot of time for RE-reading.

Now how can annotating (a couple words per paragraph) or underlining while reading help you?

Have you ever read through a passage knowing that you actually read every word, but when you are done reading the passage you have NO IDEA what you just read about?!?! That happens ALL the time on these boring passages. The best way to focus while you are reading is to focus on one paragraph at a time. Read the paragraph and then write down one or two words in the margins of what you thought the main idea was. Now it doesn't need to be a complete sentence - it is just for you! The is especially important to do on the passages that you don't understand at all. It will help you get through the reading! In fact, you almost want to think about it as making a reverse outline of the essay: try to imagine what the author had in his/her original outline before he/she wrote the passage. Take out all the fluff (transitions and details) and focus on what the main ideas are.

Annotating can also save you time on the test. By reading the passage once closely and annotating, you will hopefully be able to save time when answering the questions. There is a good chance when you read the question, you will know where to find the answer in the passage. If you aren't sure exactly where to look, use your annotations to help!

2. Read the question and predict your answer.

Reading the whole passage and annotating doesn't get you any points on the tests, so now it is time for the questions. This is where the key to the reading strategy comes into play. It does take some practice though because it is so easy to just take a peek at the answer choices. You want to read the question WITHOUT looking at the answers. If you need to, cover the answer choices with your hand. You want to answer the question in your own words.

How do you know where to look to make the prediction?

This is one of the best parts of the reading test – it is OPEN BOOK! You are supposed to look back at the passage to find the answers. You can use your ANNOTATIONS to know where in the passage you need to look to find the answer!

What about questions that give you line numbers?

Even better! They are telling you where to find the answer! You should reread the passage starting a couple lines above where they tell you to look down to a couple lines past where they tell you to stop. You need to make sure you are getting a feel for what they are asking about in the context of the passage in order to help you with your prediction.

What if you have no idea for a prediction?

If you can't come up with a prediction, try to at least have an idea of what you are looking for. For example, if the question is, "What were the character's feelings about the day that she had?" If you are not sure how the character felt, but you know that bad things were happening, that is good enough for a prediction. There will be some questions that you absolutely CANNOT come up with a prediction for, and in that case, go ahead and look at the answer choices.

3. Pick the answer that best matches your prediction.

After you have a prediction, go through the answer choices and choose the answer that is closest to your prediction. The idea behind coming up with a prediction before you look at the answer choices is that you are matching IDEAS about the passage instead of matching WORDS that appear in the passage. There are many wrong answer choices that accurately reflect what took place in the passage, but they are the choice because they don't answer what the question is asking

Sometimes your prediction will be almost one of the answer choices word for word. Sometimes your prediction will not come close the any of the answer choices, but in that case, hopefully your prediction can help you eliminate wrong answer choices.

How can eliminating answer choices help you?

The more answer choices you can eliminate, the closer you are to the correct answer! Sometimes you may not know why the right answer choice is the correct answer, but you may know that the other three choices have to be wrong!

Reading Timing and Scoring

It is especially important to keep in mind the timing for the reading section because even if you are a fast reader, the time can fly by in this section. Some important tips to keep in mind:

• Do your easy passage first.
• If you don't have time to read all 4 passages:
  • Plan on only reading 3 of the 4 passages.
    o Use the strategy discussed above for 3 of the passages.
    o If you plan on only 3 passages, instead of having 8.5 minutes per passage, you will now have 11 minutes per passage!
    o On the 4th passage, you will have most likely have less than 5 minutes.
  • It is a good idea to save the Paired Passage for last (the passage that contains Passage A and Passage B)
    o See which passage has more questions.
      ▪ Read that passage and answer the questions for the passage
      • Take your best guess on the questions about both passages!
  ▪ If you save a DIFFERENT passage for last:
    • DON'T READ THE PASSAGE FIRST
    • Start with the questions that have line number references. Read to find the answers to these questions.
    • Guess the same letter on the remaining questions
    • Try to answer questions with whatever time you have remaining.

*If you do well on the 3 passages you do read, and do some educated guessing on the 4th passage, it is possible to score in the **high 20s** on the reading section!*

Reading and Annotating

Now time to jump into reading an actual passage! On the next page, there is a passage that we are going to read, and then the rest of the reading section is going to have questions relating to this passage. As I mentioned already, almost all of the passages on the reading test are pretty boring. Annotating one or two words per paragraph is the best way to fight the boredom!

There is no right or wrong answer as you are annotating, just whatever you think the main idea of the paragraph is!

Go ahead, read the passage. On the page following the passage, I'll write out my annotations so that you can get an idea of how I would approach it.

Try to keep in mind that you want to figure out what the author's outline might have looked like!

Peter Lovesey is a novelist, best known as creator of the Victorian cop, 'Cribb', and one of Britain's leading athletics historians, author of The Official Centenary History Of The Amateur Athletic Association (1979). His website: peterlovesey.com. The article on the next page is an adaptation of one first appearing in the Journal of Olympic History, v.10 (2002).

There have been many exciting Olympic contests, but the 1908 race which came to be known as Dorando's marathon has passed into legend as the most heart-rending. The image of the exhausted Italian runner being assisted across the finish line and so disqualified appears in almost every history of the Games. This was an extraordinary event. Queen Alexandra was so touched by the harrowing scenes in the stadium that she presented a special cup to Dorando Pietri. Irving Berlin wrote a song called Dorando. The King had a horse named after the runner. And a craze for marathon-running was born.

But now let us dispose of a *canard*. For years there has been a story that Sir Arthur Conan Doyle, the creator of Sherlock Holmes, was one of the officials who assisted Dorando at the finish of the 1908 Olympic marathon and so made the disqualification inevitable. He has even been identified as a portly figure in a straw boater pictured in the background of one of the most famous of all Olympic photographs. Sadly for the romantics, the story isn't true. The two officials at either side of the athlete are Jack Andrew, the Clerk of the Course, holding the megaphone, and Dr Michael Bulger, the chief medical officer. The man in the background (and seen beside the stricken Pietri in other photos) is probably another of the medical team. Conan Doyle was seated in the stands.

His report in the Daily Mail (25 July, 1908) makes this clear.

Then again he collapsed, kind hands saving him from a heavy fall. He was within a few yards of my seat. Amid stooping figures and grasping hands I caught a glimpse of the haggard, yellow face, the glazed, expressionless eyes, the lank black hair streaked across the brow.

Conan Doyle had been commissioned by Lord Northcliffe to write a special report of the race. "I do not often do journalistic work," he recalled in his memoirs, "but on the occasion of the Olympic Games of 1908 I was tempted, chiefly by the offer of an excellent seat, to do the Marathon Race for the 'Daily Mail'." The almost melodramatic scenes affected him deeply. "It is horrible, and yet fascinating, this struggle between a set purpose and an utterly exhausted frame." Nothing like it had been seen to that time, though similar scenes would occur at marathon finishes in the future. With remarkable foresight, Conan Doyle finished his report with the words, "The Italian's great performance can never be effaced from our records of sport, be the decision of the judges what it may."

It has been suggested that the cup presented next day by Queen Alexandra was Conan Doyle's idea, but this is another distortion of the truth. In fact, Conan Doyle's contribution was financial; he got up a fund to raise money for Dorando Pietri. A letter published beside his report in the Daily Mail stated:

I am sure that no petty personal recompense can in the least console Dorando for the national loss which follows from his disqualification. Yet I am certain that many who saw his splendid effort in the Stadium, an effort which ran him within an inch of his life, would like to feel that he carries away some souvenir from his admirers in England. I should be very glad to contribute five pounds to such a fund if any of the authorities at the Stadium would consent to organise it.

Nobody seemed to bother that Dorando's amateur status might be sullied. The appeal raised the substantial sum of £308. Readers of the paper were informed that the money would be used to enable the gallant runner to start up as a baker in his own village. If the villagers were relying on him for bread, they must have been disappointed. He turned professional and cashed in on the marathon craze triggered by his race. For much of the next year he was in the United States, only returning to Italy in May, 1909. His travels lasted until 1912.

For Conan Doyle, that hot afternoon in the White City Stadium was an epiphany that convinced him of the international significance of the Olympic movement. As an all-round sportsman, he was quite an Olympian himself. Between 1900 and 1907, he played cricket for the MCC, was a useful slow bowler and once took the wicket of the finest batsman of the century, W.G.Grace. He was a founder of Portsmouth Football Club (1884) playing in goal and as a defender until he was forty-four; had a golf handicap of ten; and in 1913 got to the third round of the British amateur billiards championship. His knowledge of boxing, particularly the prize-ring, is evident in his writing, particularly Rodney Stone and The Croxley Master. And he is often credited with popularising skiing during the years he spent in Switzerland. A plaque celebrating his part in the history of Swiss skiing can be seen at Davos.

http://publicdomainreview.org/2012/08/09/conan-doyles-olympic-crusade/

My annotations:

Paragraph 1: Dorando Olympic runner

Paragraph 2: Doyle didn't help runner

Paragraph 3: Doyle's words re: race

Paragraph 4: Doyle went for great seat

Paragraph 5: Doyle raised $

Paragraph 6: $ to console Dorando

Paragraph 7: $ for bakery but ran instead

Paragraph 8: Doyle plays sports

Now remember, there is no right or wrong answer for the annotations! This is what I came up with when I read it, but if I read it 10 times, I will probably have different annotations each time.

Reading is important, but it is answering questions that will get you the points. Let's take a look at the different types of questions that you are going to come across.

Key Ideas and Details

Locate Significant Details

Some questions will tell you exactly where to look to find the answer by providing you line numbers to reference. When they do, read the lines the question directs you to as well as a few lines above it and a few lines below it. The correct answer might not be a word for word match, but it will have the same idea as what is talked about.

BEWARE: some of the wrong answer choices might use words that are in the passage, but the meaning won't be the same.

On this page, I am going to write my predictions to the answers, but I'll put the answer choices on the next page. It is difficult to get in the habit of putting the answer in your own words before you look at the answer choices, but I promise if you practice and work on doing this, you will be able to answer the questions faster and more accurately than by just looking at the answer choices to start with.

1. Who asked Sir Arthur Conan Doyle to write a special report for the Daily Mail?

    My thought process for this prediction is that I think they talked about writing the special report in paragraphs 3 and 4, so I'll skim these paragraphs looking for who asked Doyle to write the report…. In the first sentence of paragraph 4 is my answer:

     Prediction: Lord Northcliffe

2. According to paragraph 7 (lines 65-75), did Dorando use the money for the purpose the readers of the paper were told it would be used for?

    Now this is telling me exactly where to look to find the answer. I'll reread that paragraph, but I'll also look at my annotations. I wrote, "$ for bakery but ran instead" as my annotation, and that is exactly what I'm going to use for my prediction.

     Prediction: $ for bakery but ran instead

3. Which of the following sports did Sir Arthur Conan Doyle NOT participate in?

This one I can't really "predict" on because I could guess all day about what Doyle didn't do. But I can "Predict" where it talked about the sports that he played:

Prediction: the last paragraph

Now it is time to match the predictions to the answer choices!

1. Who asked Sir Arthur Conan Doyle to write a special report for the Daily Mail?
   Prediction: Lord Northcliffe

   A. Dorando Pietri
   B. Jack Andrew
   C. Lord Northcliffe
   D. Queen Alexandra

   C is the EXACT same as prediction, and it is the right answer.

2. According to paragraph 7 (lines 65-75), did Dorando use the money for the purpose the readers of the paper were told it would be used for?
   Prediction: $ for bakery but ran instead

   F. Yes, Dorando used the money to start up as a baker in his own village.
   G. Yes, Dorando used the money to pay for running marathons.
   H. No, Dorando used the money to open a bakery instead.
   J. No, Dorando turned into a professional marathon runner instead.

   The answer to the question has to be no, so F and G are out. When I look at what I predicted and try to match it to H or J, J is the better match, so that is what I will choose. And it just happens to be the correct answer.

3. Which of the following sports did Sir Arthur Conan Doyle NOT participate in?

   Prediction: last paragraph.

    A.   cricket

    B.   marathon running

    C.   skiing

    D.   billiards

According to the last paragraph, Doyle played cricket, billiards, football and boxing. Since marathon running is NOT in the list, B is the answer.

Practice Problems:

Red Book Test 2	Red Book Test 3	Red Book Test 4	Red Book Test 5
2, 3, 5, 6, 8, 10	1, 3, 5, 7, 8, 9, 10	1, 4, 5, 7, 9, 10	4, 9, 10
11, 12, 16, 19, 20	12, 14, 15, 17, 19	12, 15, 17, 19	11, 13, 15, 16
23, 24, 25	22, 23, 27, 28, 29, 30	21, 24, 25, 26, 27, 29, 30	21, 26, 27, 28
37, 38, 39, 40	32, 34, 35, 36, 37, 40	37, 38, 40	33, 35, 36, 37

Determine Main Ideas

Main idea questions are just like they sound; you need to figure out what the overall question is asking about. I do have one warning for you for main idea questions. The wrong answers might very well have been discussed in the paragraph or passage that the question is asking about. What will make the wrong answers wrong though is that they will pick only one DETAIL that was discussed. These questions will be SO much easier if you annotated while you were reading!

One other piece of advice for main idea questions is that it is very common for the test to place a question about the main idea of a passage as the first question about the passage. It is easier to answer this question after you go through all the questions about the passage because then you have a better idea of what ACT thinks the main idea of the passage is!

4. What is the main idea of the letter (lines 56-64) that was published next to Doyle's article?

    Prediction:

5. The main idea of paragraph one (lines 1-12) is:

    Prediction:

4. What is the main idea of the letter (lines 56-64) that was published next to Doyle's article?

    F. Doyle himself donated 5 pounds to the cause.
    G. To give the reader of the newspaper a way to help Dorando.
    H. To discuss a souvenir for Dorando's fans.
    J. To pay Dorando's disqualification fees.

    My prediction for paragraph 6 was, "$ to console Dorando," which goes hand in hand with G. If you chose F, H, or J, then you were looking at details or words used in the paragraph, but not the overarching main idea.

5. The main idea of paragraph one (lines 1-12) is:

    A. Queen Alexandra presented a special cup to Dorando Pietri
    B. Everyone wanted to run marathons.
    C. The 1908 Olympic race was the most exciting in the history of the Olympics.
    D. Dorando Pietri ran in the 1908 Olympics and was the subject of a famous

        photograph due to the fact that he was assisted across the finish line.

Surprise, surprise. We are going back to the annotations that we wrote down while reading. For the first paragraph, I wrote, "Dorando Olympic runner". That is my prediction. The answer that is closest to that is D and that is the correct answer. Just like number 6, if you chose one of the other choices, you fell for the trap of choosing answer choices that have wording that appears in the paragraph but isn't the main idea.

Red Book Test 2	Red Book Test 3	Red Book Test 4	Red Book Test 5
17, 21, 22, 27, 31, 34	11	13, 14, 22	5, 12, 22, 32, 34

Sequence of Events

Sequence of event questions can be a little tricky because these questions are usually only asked if the sequence of events doesn't necessarily match when the events are written about in the passage. You most likely will have to refer back to the passage to figure out what the sequence is, and make sure to look out for timing keywords such as *then*, *before*, and *after*!

6. Which of the following took place first?

Prediction:

What?!? Can you predict for this one? No, you can't predict. You would be guessing all day long. You just need to read through the answer choices and refer for the passage. Remember that the question is asking about the timing of events and not necessarily the order in which they are discussed in the passage.

    F.   Doyle wrote the article for the paper.
    G.   Doyle played cricket.
    H.   The marathon that is referenced in the first paragraph.
    J.   Doyle founded the Portsmouth Football Club.

The easiest thing to do is to skim through the passage and try to reference dates when available.

    F.   Doyle wrote the article for the paper. (1908)
    G.   Doyle played cricket. (1900-1907)
    H.   The marathon that is referenced in the first paragraph. (1908)
    J.   Doyle founded the Portsmouth Football Club (1884)

When you find the dates of the events listed, it is obvious that choice J is the correct answer.

Red Book Test 2	Red Book Test 3	Red Book Test 4	Red Book Test 5
33	None	None	None

Craft and Structure

Vocabulary in Context

The easiest way to approach vocab questions is to simply plug the answer choices in for the word that you are trying to replace. As for difficult vocab throughout the reading passage, try to figure out if the word sounds positive, negative, or neutral. A lot of times the "feeling" that you get from a word can help you understand what it means. You know a lot more about the English language than you think you do!

For example, do you know what *haughty* means? Does is look like something good or bad? To me, it looks like naughty, so I think that it looks bad. It actually means "arrogant", so it is bad!

Does a word look positive, negative, or neutral? Use this thought process when you don't know what a word means.

7. The word *canard* in line 13 can be replaced with which of the following?
Prediction:

7. The word *canard* in line 13 can be replaced with which of the following?

If I read the full paragraph, in the next sentence, it refers to a story. As I keep reading, the essay states, "the story isn't true," so that would be my prediction.

Prediction: the story isn't true

    A.   false story

    B.   duck

    C.   accurate tale

    D.   romantic story

A is the correct answer. C is the opposite meaning, B is another meaning for the word canard, and D uses another word that appears in the paragraph, but in the wrong context.

Red Book Test 2	Red Book Test 3	Red Book Test 4	Red Book Test 5
15	18, 20, 25, 33, 38, 39	2, 11, 19, 28, 35, 39	6, 25, 30, 40

Author Purpose

Author's purpose questions are just like they sound. The test is going to ask you questions about why the author decided to include certain information in the passage. The best way to answer this is to read a couple lines above and a couple lines below where the question is asking about!

For line number questions, read a couple lines above and a couple lines below the lines noted.

8. Why did the author include Doyle's report (Lines 30 – 34) in this passage?
Prediction:

The annotations for the previous paragraph and this paragraph were Doyle didn't help runner and Doyle's words re: race. When I reread Lines 30-34, Doyle is talking about what he saw from where he was sitting.

Prediction: What Doyle saw from where he was sitting

A. To prove the Doyle did help the runner.
B. To give the reader an idea of what Doyle was feeling while at the race.
C. To prove using Doyle's own words that he was not one of the officials.
D. To describe the appearance of the runner.

A states the opposite of what happened in the passage. B is wrong because the passage doesn't refer to Doyle's feelings. D is wrong because although this paragraph does describe the appearance of the runner, the answer does not tell you why the author included this paragraph in this passage. C is the correct answer.

Red Book Test 2	Red Book Test 3	Red Book Test 4	Red Book Test 5
4, 13, 14, 35	2, 16	31	None

Rhetorical Devices and Literary Techniques

Rhetorical devices and literary techniques are structures used by writers to help convey their message in a simple manner to the readers. There are two main types: elements and techniques.

Elements are things such as plot, setting, narrative structure, characters, mood, theme, etc.

Techniques are what writers use to enable readers to have a deeper understanding of their literary works. Some examples of techniques are metaphor, simile, alliteration, etc.

9. Which of the following words is used more literally than figuratively?

Prediction: Can't really predict on this one. You just need to read through the answer choices.

You need to read the answer choices, and look at each word in the context that it is being used in the passage.

    A.   touched (Line 8)
    B.   dispose (Line 13)
    C.   collapsed (Line 30)
    D.   struggle (Line 42)

When you look at each of the answer choices in context, "touched," "dispose," and "struggle" are all being used figuratively. In other words, no one *touched* Queen Alexandra. The correct answer is C because the runner did collapse.

Red Book Test 2	Red Book Test 3	Red Book Test 4	Red Book Test 5
9, 32	4, 13, 21	3, 16	2, 23

Text Structure

When the author is writing a passage, there are infinite possibilities for the structure of the passage, so there is a reason why the author formats the passage the way that he/she does.

10. Which of the following statements best describes the structure of this passage?

Prediction:

    I need to go back and look at my annotations to form my prediction:
      Paragraph 1: Dorando Olympic runner

      Paragraph 2: Doyle didn't help runner

Paragraph 3: Doyle's words re: race

Paragraph 4: Doyle went for great seat

Paragraph 5: Doyle raised $

Paragraph 6: $ to console Dorando

Paragraph 7: $ for bakery but ran instead

Paragraph 8: Doyle played sports

I thought the passage was mainly about Doyle, and the passage started off with a story about the Olympics and a story that was not true about Doyle. It then went through more information about Doyle and ended talking about the Olympics again.

10. Which of the following statements best describes the structure of this passage?

    A.   It begins and ends with inaccuracies about the Olympics that surround a story used by the narrator.

    B.   It contains a highly detailed story about the Olympics and what took place with one runner that was disqualified.

    C.   It contains a story about a recent event in Sir Author Conan Doyle's life.

    D.   It begins with an widely held belief story regarding Sir Author Conan Doyle, and then goes on to talk about various aspects of Doyle's life.

The answer choice that is closest to my prediction is D. Would you be surprised if I said that it is the right answer? It is!

Red Book Test 2	Red Book Test 3	Red Book Test 4	Red Book Test 5
None	None	None	31

Integration of Knowledge and Ideas

Draw Generalizations

Drawing generalization questions are going to ask you to read "between the lines" of the passage. You are going to be able to find evidence in the passage for the correct answer, which is why you still want to Predict on these questions. In fact, predicting is going to make answering these questions MUCH easier!

11. Why was Dorando Pietri disqualified during the Olympic marathon?

Prediction:

11. Why was Dorando Pietri disqualified during the Olympic marathon?

Prediction: It talked about Dorando's disqualification in the first paragraph. The passage states that there is a picture of "the exhausted Italian runner being assisted across the finish line and so disqualified."

F.   Dorando had heart issues.
G.   Sir Authur Conan Doyle helped Dorando across the finish line.
H.   Dorando was too exhausted to finish the race on his own.
J.   Dorando wanted to set up a bakery in his hometown.

Going through the answer choices without an idea in mind can get very confusing. The passage actually uses similar wording or references all of the wrong answer choices, which it is why it is easier to try and match ideas.

The passage implies that Dorando was too tired to finish the race. Choice H.

Practice Problems:

Red Book Test 2	Red Book Test 3	Red Book Test 4	Red Book Test 5
1, 7, 18, 26, 36	6, 24, 26, 31	6, 18, 20, 23, 32, 33, 34	1, 3, 7, 8, 14, 17, 24, 29, 38, 39

Comparisons Between Passages

One of the passages on each test is a Paired Passage. What that means is that there are going to be two smaller passages that relate to each other in some way – either by topic or author. It is going to be obvious which questions go with which passage because they are marked very clearly. Several questions will be about Passage A, several about Passage B, and then a couple of questions will compare the two passages.

The game plan for attacking this passage is to:

1. Look at the passages to see which passage (A or B) has more questions.
2. Read the Passage with MORE questions.
3. Answer the questions for that passage.
4. If you are short on time, try the questions about both passages and then guess the same letter for the rest of the questions.
5. If you are not short on time, read the other passage.
6. Answer the questions for the other passage.
7. Answer the questions comparing the two passages.

Red Book Test 2	Red Book Test 3	Red Book Test 4	Red Book Test 5
28, 29, 30	None	8, 36	18, 19, 20

SCIENCE

POINT

LITERALLY POINT TO
WHERE THE QUESTION IS
TELLING YOU WHERE TO
FIND THE ANSWER

There are 6 or 7 passages on the Science test, and the passages appear in a **random** order on every test.

Data Representation:

> 2 passages
> 6 questions each
> Mostly graphs and tables- the likes of which you have never seen before!

Research Summary:

> 3 passages
> 7 questions each
> You will see headings such as Study 1, Study 2, or Experiment 1, Experiment 2.
> There is more text in these passages, but there are still graphs and tables.
> It is organized like lab reports that you may have written in school.
>> The purpose and hypothesis are in the first paragraph. Directly following the headings for the studies or experiments is a description of the methods used. The passage ends with the results.

Conflicting Viewpoints:

> 1 passage
> 7 questions
> 2 or more scientists or students are fighting over a viewpoint on a specific scientific topic.
> You'll either like this passage because it is like the reading test, or you will hate it because it is like the reading test!

You have a total of 35 minutes for Science, and with 6 passages, that means you have about 5 minutes per passage.

Just like on the Reading test, to get the most points, do your "easy" passages first. Remember that the passages are not in the same order on every test, so that means that you might need to skip passages to get to your "easy" passages first.

It is also important to know that the questions are not in order of difficulty. So just like on the Reading test, if you get stuck on a question, try doing the other questions in that passage and then look at the hard question again. Because all the questions in a passage are about the same information, sometimes other questions can give you a hint!

5 topics appear on the science test:

Biology

Chemistry

Physics

Earth Science

Space Science

There are only 1-4 questions on the entire test that require background science knowledge.

Common topics that appear on the test that require science knowledge are usually in Chemistry or Biology. pH is a topic that is often on the test. pH of 7 is neutral, less than 7 is acidic, and greater than 7 is basic. Occasionally, you will need to understand how to balance chemical equations, or you might need to know that neutrons and protons are in a nucleus. For a Biology question, they might ask you about what process takes place in an organ, or you might need to know that the sun gives off the most intense solar radiation at noon. No matter what the science knowledge questions are, studying a science text book is NOT going to help you for the test. The topics that appear vary so much, and there are so few questions that require science knowledge that you really shouldn't worry about it! If you know what the answer is, go for it! If you have no idea what the answer is, take your best guess and keep moving through the test!

Game Plan for Science

1. *Look at the heading and labels on the graphs and tables. (Read as little as possible).*

2. *Read the question slowly and POINT to where the question is telling you to look.*

3. *If you know the answer, go for it! If you don't, eliminate!*

I break the remaining questions into two categories:

- 2/3 of the questions (about 25 questions) are what I call *Pointing Questions*. This is just what it sounds like. Pointing at the graphs and tables will get you to the right answer!
- The remaining 1/3 of the questions (about 12 questions) are what I call *Thinking Questions*. These are usually harder than the *Pointing Questions* because they require thinking like a scientist versus just using the information that is in the tables and graphs.

Game Plan for Science

1. Look at the headings and label on the figures and tables. (Don't read the text!)

Why should you read as little as possible?

There is a good chance that you will be burnt out on reading, especially when coming from the reading test. Like I mentioned already, 2/3 of the questions on the Science test are about looking at the graphs and tables. This means that spending a lot of time reading and trying to understand the design of the experiments might just be wasted time!

Why look at the tables and figures before going to the questions?

Some students LOVE to go directly to the questions without looking at anything in the passage, but I think it is worth taking a few seconds to look at the heading and labels of the figures and tables. It is pretty much guaranteed that the labels on the tables and graphs will show up in the questions, so when they do, you will be able to find the answers faster.

How much time should you spend looking at the tables and the graphs?

I only spend about 30 seconds looking at the graphs and the tables. You don't want to take the time to analyze trends or figure out how the experiment is set up. It isn't worth wasting time on this because there is a good chance you WON'T have a question about it!

What about the conflicting viewpoint (or fighting scientists) passage?

Unfortunately, this is the ONE passage you do have to read! I'll give you a special game plan just for this passage (See page 159).

2. Read the question <u>slowly</u> and <u>POINT</u> to where the question tells you to look.

Why is it important to read the questions carefully?

It is very common for the questions on the Science section to contain information you need to get the question correct.

Another reason is that many students read the question quickly the first time, and then go back and read the question slower trying to understand what the question is asking. If you read the question slowly the first time, you will only have to read the question once (an EASY way to save some time!)

What do I mean by POINT?

It might sound silly, but I mean to literally POINT to where the question is telling you to look. For example, in Figure 1 (I would put my finger on Figure 1) when the average steps per day (I would put my finger on average steps per day) increases (I would move my finger from left to right because the number of steps are getting bigger), what happens to the average resting heart rate?

Before you even look at the answer choices, you can see that as you moved your finger from left to right, the line for the average resting heart rate is going down – so I would say that it decreases!

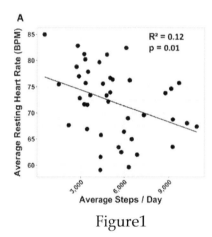

Figure1

(http://journals.plos.org/plosbiology/article?id=10.1371/journal.pbio.2001402)

Can you POINT for every question?

Unfortunately, no you can't. Remember I said that 2/3 of the questions (or about 25 questions) are pointing questions. For the Pointing Questions, this should be all you have to do. Some of the questions might be harder and require looking at 2 tables or graphs, but these pointing questions are pretty straightforward.

If you can't POINT, then you have a Thinking Question. Even though you can't point to an answer, the thinking questions still give you a hint about where to look to find the answer. You will need to read the passage for these questions, but the hint will give you some direction as to where to look in the passage. What do I mean by hint? For example, if the question is about a step in Experiment 1, you will need to read the method for Experiment 1. You don't need to read the entire thing; you just need to read to find the answer.

2. **If you know the answer, go for it. If you are stuck, eliminate answer choices that you know are wrong.**

If it was a POINTING question, and you know what the answer is, go for it! Answer and move on the next question. If you don't know the answer, eliminate what you know has to be wrong. The Science test is notorious for the questions that look like:

> A. Yes, reason 1
> B. Yes, reason 2
> C. No, reason 1
> D. No, reason 2

These questions can be tricky and elimination is going to be your best friend on these! Answer yes or no first, and then only look at those two answer choices. If you have no idea, the reason is usually easier to understand than what the question is asking, so you can also use the reason to eliminate answer choices!

If it was a Thinking question, you won't know the answer by the time you are doing reading the question, but you will need to go back and read in the passage to get the answer. The good thing about Science compared to Reading is that the questions in the science test are REALLY straightforward if you can get over all the science speak!

Science Timing and Scoring

You have a total of 35 minutes for Science, and with 6-7 passages, that means you have about 5 minutes per passage.

The science test does not have questions in order of difficulty within a passage; if you are stuck on a question, move on to the next one. Make sure you have enough time to get all of the easy questions on the test!

Some important tips to keep in mind:

- Do you easy passage first.
- If you don't have time to complete all 6-7 passages:
  - Plan on saving the conflicting viewpoints (or fighting scientists) for last.
  - When you get to the conflicting viewpoints passage, you can decide what to do based on time.
  - If you have 5 minutes remaining:
    - Skim through the questions to see which scientist has the most questions asked about him/her.
    - Read the first paragraph and the viewpoint of the scientist that has the most questions asked about him/her.
    - Answer the questions for that scientist and take your best guess on the questions about all of the scientists based off of what you know from reading about one scientist.
  - If you have less than 5 minutes, fill in all the answers on your sheet with the same letter, and then follow the directions for 5 minutes remaining to try to get a couple of questions correct. On Science, every additional question you get right can increase your score one point!

Now let's practice!

Passage I

Adapted from Revised Estimates for the Number of Human and Bacteria Cells in the Body, written by Ron Sender, Shai Fuchs, Ron Milo. Published: August 19, 2016
http://journals.plos.org/plosbiology/article?id=10.1371/journal.pbio.1002533

How many cells are there in the human body? Beyond order of magnitude statements that give no primary reference or uncertainty estimates, very few detailed estimates have been performed (the one exception is discussed below). Similarly, the ubiquitous statements regarding 10^{14}–10^{15} bacteria residing in our body trace back to an old back-of-the-envelope calculation.

Microbes are found throughout the human body, mainly on the external and internal surfaces, including the gastrointestinal tract, skin, saliva, oral mucosa, and conjunctiva. Bacteria overwhelmingly outnumber eukaryotes and archaea in the human microbiome by 2–3 orders of magnitude. We therefore sometimes operationally refer to the microbial cells in the human body as bacteria. The diversity in locations where microbes reside in the body makes estimating their overall number daunting. Yet, once their quantitative distribution shows the dominance of the colon as discussed below, the problem becomes much simpler. The vast majority of the bacteria reside in the colon, with previous estimates of about 10^{14} bacteria, followed by the skin, which is estimated to harbor ~10^{12} bacteria.

Table 1 shows typical order of magnitude estimates for the number of bacteria that reside in different organs in the human body. The estimates are based on multiplying measured concentrations of bacteria by the volume of each organ. Values are rounded up to give an order of magnitude upper bound.

Location	Typical concentration of bacteria [1] (number/mL content)	Volume (mL)	Order of magnitude bound for bacteria number
Colon (large intestine)	10^{11}	400 [2]	10^{14}
Dental plaque	10^{11}	<10	10^{12}
Ileum (lower small intestine)	10^{8}	400 [5]	10^{11}
Saliva	10^{9}	<100	10^{11}
Skin	<10^{11} per m^2 [3]	1.8 m^2 [4]	10^{11}
Stomach	10^{3}–10^{4}	250 [5]–900 [6]	10^{7}
Duodenum and Jejunum (upper small intestine)	10^{3}–10^{4}	400 [5]	10^{7}

[1] Except for skin, concentrations are according to [9]. For the skin, we used bacterial areal density and total skin surface to reach an upper bound.

[2] See derivation in section below.

[3] Skin surface bacteria density is taken from [11].

[4] Skin area calculated as inferred from standard formula by DuBois for the body surface area [12].

[5] Volume of the organs of the gastrointestinal tract is derived from weights taken from [13] by assuming content density of 1.04 g/mL [6].

[6] Higher value is given in [14].

doi:10.1371/journal.pbio.1002533.t001

Table 1. Bounds for bacteria number in different organs, derived from bacterial concentrations and volume.

It is prudent in making such estimates to approach the analysis from different angles. In that spirit, we now ask does the cumulative mass of the cells counted fall within the expected range for a reference adult? To properly tackle that question, we first need to state what the anticipated result is, i.e., total body cell mass. For a reference man mass of 70 kg, 25% is extracellular fluid, another 7% is extracellular solids, thus we need to account for ≈46 kg of cell mass (including fat).

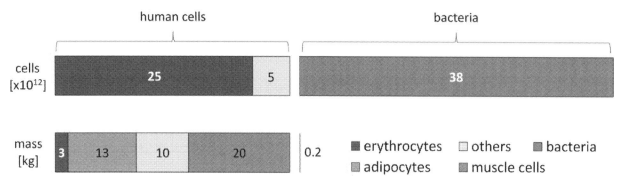

Fig 1. Distribution of cell number and mass for different cell types in the human body (for a 70 kg adult man).

Interpretation of Data

Graph Reading

Graph reading questions are at the heart of the Point strategy. About 26 out of the 40 questions are going to ask you to read from a graph or table to find the information.

Let's walk through a science question together systematically. On the previous page is a science passage.

Step 1. Look at the headings and labels of the graphs and tables.

Table 1 shows the *Location, Typical concentration of bacteria, Volume*, and *Order of magnitude bound for bacteria number*. Figure 1 shows the *Cells and mass for human cells and bacteria*.

That is EVERYTHING I want you to look at before going to the questions! Don't look for trends! Don't try to understand what is going on! Save time and energy by just looking at the headings and labels.

Step 2. Read the question slowly and POINT to where the question tells you to look.

I want to show you how I break a question down step by step.

According to Figure 1, *(I would now put my finger on Figure 1)*

is the concentration of bacteria *(I would put by finger on Typical Concentration of Bacteria)*

higher in the stomach or colon? *(I would put by finger on stomach and colon)*

If you break down the question step by step, there is good chance you are pointing at the answer when you are done reading the question! Which has the higher concentration – stomach or colon?

Example 1. According to Figure 1, is the concentration of bacteria higher in the stomach or colon?

    A. Stomach, because the concentration is $10^3 - 10^4$ in the stomach and it is 10^{11} in the colon.

    B. Stomach, because the concentration is 10^{11} in the stomach and it is $10^3 - 10^4$ in the colon.

    C. Colon, because the concentration is $10^3 - 10^4$ in the stomach and it is 10^{11} in the colon.

    D. Colon, because the concentration is 10^{11} in the stomach and it is $10^3 - 10^4$ in the colon.

It is easiest to answer the question first, and then to look at the reasoning. If you followed through with what we went through step by step, then you know the answer has to be colon. Why? Because the colon had more bacteria. 10^{11} is a 1 with 11 zeros after it. That is a lot of bacteria! So the answer is D.

Let's try another example. This time I am not going to walk through the problem step by step. I am just going to give you the question as an example, and then I will explain it in the answer. Even though I am not walking through it step by step, I HIGHLY recommend that you do, in order to help with the accuracy and speed of answering the question!

Example 2. The typical concentration of bacteria, shown in Figure 1, for dental plaque is most similar to which location of the human body?

    F. Colon
    G. Ileum
    H. Saliva
    J. Stomach

The easiest way to answer this question is to read slowly and point to where the question is telling you to look. Look at the typical concentration of bacteria column in Figure 1. Next, the question tells you to look at dental plaque, and the question is asking what is closest to the value for dental plaque. When you look at the figure, colon has the same value, so colon must be the correct answer. It is choice F.

Practice Problems:

Red Book Test 2	Red Book Test 3	Red Book Test 4	Red Book Test 5
1, 2, 3, 4, 5, 35, 36, 38, 40	1, 2, 3, 4, 5, 6, 7, 8, 9, 12, 21	14, 15, 17, 19, 20, 22, 24, 27, 28, 32, 33, 34, 35, 40	4, 6, 7, 8, 9, 15, 16, 17, 18, 27, 28

Interpretation of Information Presented

The interpretation of information questions are still pointing questions, but they tend to be a bit harder. You want to follow the same process that we have been going through, but you might need to understand how topics relate to one another. Sometimes, the hardest thing to figure out is what the question is asking you. Let me show you what I mean.

As the surface area of a solvent increases, the rate at which the solvent dissolves increases and the time it takes to dissolve decreases. Powder has a higher surface area than tablets. Sam has two glasses of water. He puts NaCl tablets into one glass and powder NaCl into a second glass. If it takes 9 seconds for the tablets to dissolve, approximately how long will it take for the power to dissolve?

Taking notes on a question like this can help you figure out what the question is asking.

The notes I would take are:

As surface area ↑, rate dissolve ↑ time ↓. Powder > tablets.

Tablets = 9, then what is the time for powder?

As the surface area increase, the time decreases. So if tablets were 9 seconds, and the powder has a high surface area, then the time needs to be lower than 9 seconds.

Let's see how this type of question appears in a passage:

Example 3. There are more bacteria cells in the human body than there are human cells. How does the mass of the bacteria cells compare to the mass of other human cells?

    A. Bacteria has a greater mass than muscle cells

    B. Bacteria has more mass than adipocytes but less mass than muscle cells.

    C. Bacteria has more mass than erythrocytes but less mass than adipocytes.

    D. Bacteria has less mass than erythrocytes.

According to Figure 1, the mass of bacteria is 0.2 kg, so it is smaller than any of the other masses. That means that D must be the correct answer. The ACT will throw a bunch of scary science words into the questions to try to confuse you – don't fall for the trap!

Practice Problems:

Red Book Test 2	Red Book Test 3	Red Book Test 4	Red Book Test 5
6	10, 30, 31, 32	1, 6, 9, 10, 11, 12, 13, 16, 18, 30	1, 3, 5, 10, 13, 14, 37, 22, 25, 37

Ready for another example passage? I am!

When you go through and read the passage below, remember that I don't want you to read! I just want you to look at the headings and labels on the figures and tables!

Evaluation of Experiment Results Passage II

Adapted from <u>Assessing "Dangerous Climate Change": Required Reduction of Carbon Emissions to Protect Young People, Future Generations and Nature</u> Authored by James Hansen, Pushker Kharecha, et al. Published: December 3, 2013 http://journals.plos.org/plosone/article?id=10.1371/journal.pone.0081648

Humans are now the main cause of changes of Earth's atmospheric composition and thus the drive for future climate change. The principal climate forcing, defined as an imposed change of planetary energy balance, is increasing carbon dioxide (CO_2) from fossil fuel emissions, much of which will remain in the atmosphere for millennia. The climate response to this forcing and society's response to climate change are complicated by the system's inertia, mainly due to the ocean and the ice sheets on Greenland and Antarctica together with the long residence time of fossil fuel carbon in the climate system. The inertia causes climate to appear to respond slowly to this human-made forcing, but further long-lasting responses can be locked in.

Atmospheric CO_2 and other GHGs have been well-measured for the past half century, allowing accurate calculation of their climate forcing. The growth rate of the GHG forcing has declined moderately since its peak values in the 1980s, as the growth rate of CH_4 and chlorofluorocarbons has slowed. Annual changes of CO_2 are highly correlated with the El Niño cycle (**Fig. 1**). The CO_2 growth rate and warming rate can be expected to increase as we move into the next El Niño, with the CO_2 growth already reaching 3 ppm/year in mid-2013. The CO_2 climate forcing does not increase as rapidly as the CO_2amount because of partial saturation of CO_2 absorption bands. The GHG forcing is now increasing at a rate of almost 0.4 W/m^2 per decade.

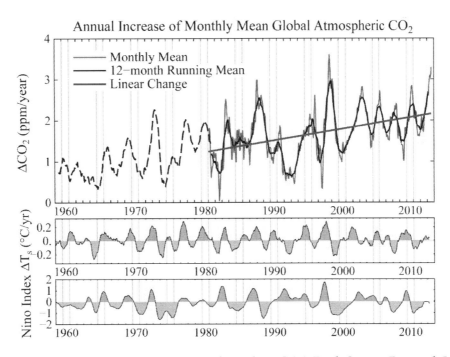

Figure 1. Annual increase of CO_2 based on data from the NOAA Earth System Research Laboratory.

Paleoclimate data are not as helpful for defining the likely rate of sea level rise in coming decades, because there is no known case of growth of a positive (warming) climate forcing as rapid as the anthropogenic change. The potential for unstable ice sheet disintegration is controversial, with opinion varying from likely stability of even the (marine) West Antarctic ice sheet to likely rapid non-linear response extending up to multi-meter sea level rise. Data for the modern rate of annual ice sheet mass changes indicate an accelerating rate of mass loss consistent with a mass loss doubling time of a decade or less (**Fig. 2**). However, we do not know the functional form of ice sheet response to a large persistent climate forcing. Longer records are needed for empirical assessment of this ostensibly nonlinear behavior.

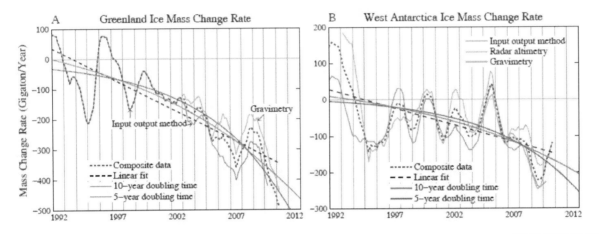

Figure 2. Annual Greenland and West Antarctic ice mass changes as estimated via alternative methods.

Interpretation of Experimental Results

In Passage II, there are some scary looking graphs! The graphs are meant to look scary. The reason that there is a Science section on the ACT is that you are being tested on whether you can look at a graph and read information from it. The interpretation questions are going to ask you to use the graphs and tables (so you can still POINT), but the questions are also going to ask you to "read" between the lines. Let me show you what I mean.

Example 4. Using the Linear Change line in Figure 1, what would the value be for ΔCO_2 in 2020?

        F. Between 0 and 1

        G. Between 1 and 2

        H. Between 2 and 3

        J. Between 3 and 4

This question isn't asking you to read a value directly off the graph. Rather it is asking you to determine if you extend the line off the graph, what would the value be for 2020? We can assume that the line continues exactly as it is on the graph. So, in 2014 the value for ΔCO_2 is already between 2 and 3. The Linear Change line is increasing, but it is increasing slowly. If I extend the line, in 2020 the value will still be between 2 and 3. If you picked H, then you picked the right answer!

Other interpretation questions might ask you to compare two graphs or tables.

Example 5. According to the Linear Fit line in Figure 2, is the Ice Mass changing faster in Greenland or West Antarctica?

      A. Greenland, because the Linear Fit line is decreasing faster for Greenland than it is for West Antarctica.

      B. West Antarctica, because the Linear Fit line is decreasing faster for West Antarctica than it is for Greenland.

      C. The Ice Mass for Greenland and West Antarctica are changing at the same rate.

      D. It cannot be determined from the information given.

When you look at the Linear Fit line in Figure 2, it is steeper for Greenland than it is for West Antarctica, so A must be the correct answer. I do want to point out that choice D, while not correct for this problem, WILL be the correct answer for some of the science questions. I wouldn't choose this answer automatically, but if you cannot figure out what the answer is from the data or the figure the question tells you to look at, don't be AFRAID to choose that answer.

Practice Problems:

Red Book Test 2	Red Book Test 3	Red Book Test 4	Red Book Test 5
8, 9, 10, 12, 13, 15, 17, 18, 19, 23, 24, 25, 27	13, 14, 15, 16, 18, 20, 22, 23, 24, 25, 26, 34, 36, 39	8, 31, 37, 38, 39	2, 11, 12, 19, 29, 31, 33, 35, 36, 40

Compare Alternate Viewpoints

The alternate viewpoint questions are always found in the Conflicting Viewpoints passage; you know, the passage that has all of the text (very rarely a table or graph) and showcases the different views of a couple people?!? I would say that this is the passage that students dislike the most. Every once in a while, I will find a student that loves this passage, but that is few and far between.

Let me start off by saying that this is a great passage to save for last. Remember that you want to get all your "easy" points first? This passage is usually the hardest because this is a passage that you actually have to read. You read that correct, but let me repeat. You must READ this passage! I know I said that the game plan is NOT to read, but this is a passage that you won't be able to get through without reading. It is made up of all Thinking Questions. If you are trying to score around a 26, I wouldn't worry too much about this passage. You are better off practicing the Pointing Questions! If you are trying to score into the 30s on Science, this passage is unavoidable!

I'm going to give you 2 game plans to approach this passage:

Plan 1 – Recommended if you have all the time in the world!

1. Start with reading the intro paragraph. The intro paragraph is going to give you the background for the topic of the passage. It is also going to give you a lot of information that the scientists must agree on. Since it is all background information, they should agree on it!
2. Next, I would read Scientist 1. The nice thing about the Science passage is that there really isn't any reading between the lines. Everything is cut and dry. In fact, you will find what each scientist thinks in the first sentence usually!
3. Now answer the questions that ask about Scientist 1.
4. Go back and read what Scientist 2 believes.
5. Answer the questions about Scientist 2.
6. Repeat this process until you have gone through all the Scientists.
7. Lastly, answer the questions that ask about more than one Scientist.

Plan 2 – Recommended if you are short on time!

1. Skim through the questions.
   a. Put a 1 next to the questions asking about Scientist 1.

b. Put a 2 next to the questions asking about Scientist 2.

c. Put a B next to the questions asking about both Scientists.

2. Read the intro paragraph and the paragraph for the Scientist that has the most questions asked about him/her. The intro paragraph is going to give you the background for the topic of the passage. It is also going to give you a lot of information that the scientists must agree on. Since it is all background information, they should agree on it!

3. Try answering ALL the questions. You will have to guess on some of the questions, but it will be an educated guess!

Practice Problems:

Red Book Test 2	Red Book Test 3	Red Book Test 4	Red Book Test 5
28, 31, 33, 34	33	2, 3, 4, 5, 7	20, 21, 23, 24, 26, 29, 31, 33, 34, 35, 36, 40

Scientific Investigation

Design of Experiments

For the Design of Experiments questions, you will need to think like a scientist. There are some vocabulary words that will show up in these questions, so let's go through and review some words that you may see on the test.

Control– This is the "unit" (whether it is a test tube, pot of plants, or whatever it may be) that the researchers didn't change. You need a control in an experiment because the control will show you what happened if you left everything as it was instead of changing whatever is being changed in the experiment.

Independent Variable – Speaking of changing things, the independent variable is what "I" change. I remember this because Independent starts with an "I". This is the variable that is on the x-axis on a graph.

Dependent Variable – This is the what is measured in the experiment. This is on the y-axis when you graph. It DEPENDS on the independent variable.

If I am running an experiment to determine if the number of Mentos that I add to a 2 Liter of Diet Coke affects the height of the geyser.

Control – I would not add any Mentos to the control bottle.

Independent variable – how many Mentos I add to each bottle.

Depending variable – how high the Diet Coke geyser is!

BTW this is a very fun experiment to do!

Design of Experiment questions might also ask you to look at things in different graphs or tables. For example, a question might ask what the difference between two trials is. This question can usually be answered just by looking at the independent variables of each trial.

Practice Problems:

Red Book Test 2	Red Book Test 3	Red Book Test 4	Red Book Test 5
7, 11, 14, 16, 20, 21, 22, 26	17, 19, 35, 37, 40	21, 23, 26, 29	30, 32, 39

Analysis

Analysis questions will ask you to take the information that is given to you in a graph or table, analyze what it means, and answer the question. Even though you might have to analyze a table, it isn't worth taking the time to do this until you have a question asking about it! Since you only have to *analyze* for a few questions, you can waste a lot of time analyzing graphs and tables that won't be asked about in the questions.

Example 6. As the Mass Change Rate becomes more negative, ice is melting faster. According to the Figure 2 in Passage II, which location, Greenland or West Antarctica, has lost more ice over the past 20 years?

F. Greenland because in 1992, the composite data shows that the Ice Change Rate was 80 Gigaton/Year.
G. Greenland because in 2010, the composite data shows that the Ice Change Rate was about -450 Gigaton/Year.
H. West Antarctica because in 1992, the composite data shows that the Ice Change Rate was 150 Gigaton/Year.
J. West Antarctica because in 2010, the composite data shows that the Ice Change Rate was -210 Gigaton/Year.

Here you have to use the information that is given to you in the question in order to analyze the graph. We are told that as the rate becomes more negative, ice is melting faster. If we are looking for which one has lost more ice, it would have to be Greenland because the numbers are more negative. For F it is true that the composite data shows that the Ice Change Rate was 80 Gigaton/Year for Greenland in the year 1992, however it doesn't explain why the Greenland has lost more ice. The answer is G because it has the correct answer to the question (Greenland) and it gives the proper reasoning.

Practice Problems:

Red Book Test 2	Red Book Test 3	Red Book Test 4	Red Book Test 5
30	27, 28, 29, 30, 33	36	None

Understanding

These are where the science knowledge questions come into play. I already mentioned that Chemistry and Biology are the two most common topics for the science knowledge questions.

pH is a common topic. A pH of 7 is neutral. pH between 1 and 7 is acidic, while pH between 7 and 14 is basic. To help you remember, think that "A" comes before "B!"

Acid	Neutral	Base
Less than 7	7	Greater than 7

I have also seen questions where you need to know that the compounds on the left of a yield sign (the arrow in the example below) for a chemical equation are reactants, and the compounds on the right are the products.

$$\text{reactants} \qquad \text{products}$$
$$2\,H_2 + O_2 \longrightarrow 2\,H_2O$$

An example of a relevant Biology knowledge would be that plants need Carbon Dioxide, sun, and water to live.

Another question that requires understanding Biology that has appeared on a couple of recent tests is:

What is the difference between a plant and an animal cell?

The answer is that a plant cell has a cell wall, while an animal cell only has a membrane.

If you understand the science, you can get a couple more questions correct on the test, but if you don't like science and have a difficult time with this section, don't worry! It is only 2-4 questions on the test! Focus on the pointing questions to get the score that you want!

Red Book Test 2	Red Book Test 3	Red Book Test 4	Red Book Test 5
29, 32, 37, 39	11, 35, 38	25	38

ESSAY (OPTIONAL)

MAKE AN OUTLINE OF WHAT YOU ARE GOING TO WRITE ABOUT

What is the writing test?

There is one writing prompt, and you have 40 minutes to plan and write your essay. It is an optional essay.

Why is the essay optional?

Not every college requires the essay score. You really need to look at the schools you are applying to in order to see if you should take the essay or not. If you are not sure where you are going to be applying, you are better off taking the essay. If a school does require an essay, they will not look at your score if you DIDN'T take the essay (even if you score a 36)!

Does the essay affect my score?

No! It is not included in your composite score at all.

How is the essay scored?

Two readers read your essay, and each reader grades the essay from 1 to 6. This means that your essay score will be from 2 to 12.

What does the essay look like?

There is a small paragraph that introduces the topic. There will then be three perspectives in relation to that topic. It doesn't matter which perspective you support, you just need to make sure you support the view that you choose and give a counterargument to the views that you do not support!

In order to get your best score on the essay, start off by carefully considering the prompt and make sure you understand the perspectives given.

Plan

After you read the paragraph and the perspectives, it is time to plan.

 *You don't need to give a counterargument for the perspective that you support, but in order to score at least an 8 on the essay, you definitely need to have counterargument for the perspectives that you don't support.*

Here is a basic outline you can use to plan:

Perspective 1:

    What is it?:

    Example:

    Counterargument:

Perspective 2:

    What is it?:

    Example:

    Counterargument:

Perspective 3:

    What is it?:

    Example:

    Counterargument:

Now it is time to fill in your outline. If you Plan like I just showed you to, you have an outline already written! You will add an introductory paragraph, in which you make your point of view well known. You will also have to add a conclusion.

When you are writing your essay:

- In your introduction, make sure the readers see that you understand the issue.
- Explain your point of view in a clear and logical way.
- If possible, discuss the issue in a broader context or evaluate the implications or complications of the issue.
- Address what others might say to refute your point of view and present a counterargument.
- Use specific examples – even if you need to make up facts!
  - Example: According to a recent study done at the University of Michigan, 95% of people who prepare for the ACT feel more confident while taking the exam.
- Vary the structure of your sentences, and use varied and precise word choices.
- Make logical relationships clear by using transitional words and phrases.
- Stay focused on the topic.
- End with a strong conclusion that summarizes or reinforces your position.

Do a final check of the essay when it is finished:

- Correct any mistakes in grammar, usage, punctuation, and spelling.
- If you find any words that are hard to read, recopy them so your readers can read them easily.
- Make any corrections and revisions neatly, between the lines (but not in the margins).

Some ideas of what you can do to get your essay started:

- If you have more ideas for the other side of the argument than you were going to support, it might be easier to support that side instead. It doesn't matter what you think in real life, just what is easier to support in your essay.
- Start your essay with a story that shows an example that supports your point of view.
- If you realize that you need more specific examples, remember that the ACT readers do not check facts. Make up a fact that supports your point of view!

It does help to read through example essays, and the best place to find those is on the ACTstudent.org website.

OVERALL TEST TIPS

 *Here are a couple of test tips that I give all of my students. Hope they help!*

- How should you fill in the answer grid?
  It sounds funny that you need to think about how to fill in an answer grid! What I recommend doing is working on two pages in the test (doing your work in the test book), and when you are done with two pages, fill in the answer grid. There are a couple reasons I recommend doing this:

  1. You get a mini-mental break after working on two pages.

  2. You can focus completely on what you are doing on the test without having to interrupt your thought process with checking to make sure you are filling in the right answer on the bubble sheet.

  3. You can go back and re-read the English section with your answers plugged in if you have them written in the test book. If you don't have your answers in the test book, you can only go back and look at the questions that you weren't sure of.

- If you don't know the answer the first time you see a question, skip it.
  You want to get all your easy points first!

  Do the rest of the page/passage and then look at the question again. If you still don't have an idea, eliminate what you can and then guess.

- If you run out of time, guess the same letter through the test.
  You can statistically score more points by picking the same letter, rather than guessing a different letter on each question if you run out of time!

TEST ANXIETY

Leading up to the Test

- Be **well prepared** for the test – which you are already doing!
- Include as much **self-testing** in your preparation as possible
- As you anticipate the exam, **think positively**, i.e., "I will do great on the ACT."; "I have studied and I do know my stuff."
- Do some serious **"thought stopping"** if you find that you are mentally comparing yourself to your peers or thinking about what your parents, friends, or anyone else may say about your performance on this exam.

The Day Before the Test

- Before you go to bed on the night before the exam, make sure to **gather anything you will need** for the exam -- pencils, eraser, calculator, ID, and admissions ticket. Double-check the time of the exam and the location (this will be found on your admission ticket!)
- Set the alarm clock and then get a **good night's sleep** before the exam!

The Day of the Test

- Get to the exam **with plenty of time.**
- **Read something before you get to the test – a magazine, a book, the newspaper, etc.**
- Don't talk to friends about the ACT just before going into the exam.
- Sit in a **location** in the exam room where you will be distracted as little as possible.
- As the papers are distributed, **calm yourself down** by closing your eyes and taking some slow deep breaths.
- As you work on the exam, **focus only on the exam**, not on what other students are doing.
- If you feel very anxious or even panicky in the test, take a time-out for a few seconds and **calm yourself down.** Stretch your arms and legs and then relax them again. Do this a couple of times. Take a few slow deep breaths. Do some positive internal self-talk; say to yourself, "I will be OK; I can do this." Then take your time and get back into the questions.
- If the exam is more difficult than you anticipated, try to **focus and just do your best** at that point. It might be enough to get you through, even with a reasonable score!

After the Test

- When the exam is over, **treat yourself!**

Relaxation Techniques

There are relaxation response techniques that you can practice leading up to the ACT and during the test These techniques will help control emotional worry and test anxiety. Once these procedures are learned, the relaxation response will take the place of an anxiety response.

THE TENSING AND DIFFERENTIAL RELAXATION METHOD
1. Put your feet flat on the floor.
2. With your hands, grab underneath the chair.
3. Push down with your feet and pull up on your chair at the same time for about five seconds.
4. Relax for five to ten seconds.
5. Repeat the procedure two or three times.
6. Relax all your muscles except the ones that are actually used to take the test.

THE PALMING METHOD

1. Close and cover your eyes using the center of the palms of your hands.
2. Prevent your hands from touching your eyes by resting the lower parts of your palms on your cheekbones and placing your fingers on your forehead. Your eyeballs must not be touched, rubbed or handled in any way.
3. Think of some real or imaginary relaxing scene. Mentally visualize this scene. Picture the scene as if you were actually there, looking through your own eyes.
4. Visualize this relaxing scene for one to two minutes.

DEEP BREATHING

1. Sit straight up in your chair in a good posture position.
2. Slowly inhale through your nose.
3. As you inhale, first fill the lower section of your belly and work your way up to the upper part of your lungs.
4. Hold your breath for a few seconds.
5. Exhale slowly through your mouth.
6. Wait a few seconds and repeat the cycle. (No one will know that you are doing this and it will be a <u>HUGE</u> help!)

Negative Self-Talk

Negative self-talk is defined as the negative statements you tell yourself before and during tests. Negative self-talk causes students to lose confidence and to give up on tests. Students need to change their negative self-talk to positive self-talk without making unrealistic statements. During tests, positive self-talk can build confidence and decrease your test anxiety. Using positive self-talk before a test can help reduce your test anxiety and improve your score.

EXAMPLES OF NEGATIVE SELF-TALK:

- "No matter what I do, I will not get a good score on the ACT."
- "I am no good at math, so why should I try?"
- "I cannot remember the answers or I have forgotten how to do the problems. I am going to fail the ACT."
- "I didn't get the score I wanted last time, and it is going to be the same this time."

EXAMPLES OF POSITIVE SELF-TALK

- "I didn't get the score I wanted last time, but I can now use my study skills to do the best I can."
- "I went blank on the last test, but now I know how to reduce test anxiety."
- "I prepared for this test and will do the best I can."
- "I feel good about myself and my abilities. I am not going to worry about that difficult problem. I'm going to use all my test time and check for careless errors. Even if I don't get the score I want on this test, it is not the end of the world."

THOUGHT-STOPPING TECHNIQUES

Some students have difficulty stopping their negative self-talk. These students cannot just tell themselves to eliminate those thoughts. These students need to use a thought-stopping technique to overcome their worry and become relaxed.

To stop your thoughts during a test, silently shout to yourself "Stop" or "Stop thinking about that." After your *silent shout*, either relax yourself or repeat one of your positive self-talk statements. You may have to *shout* to yourself several times during a test to control negative self-talk. After every shout, use a different relaxation technique/scene or positive self-talk statement.

Thought stopping works because it interrupts the worry response before it can cause high anxiety or negative emotions. During the interruption, you can replace negative self-talk with positive self-talk statements or relaxation. If you have high test anxiety, you should practice this technique three days to one week before taking the test.

Questions to ask yourself?

What is your plan to achieve your goal?

When are you going to practice?

Where are you going to practice?

Are you registered for the test?

When are you taking the test for the first time?

When are you going to take the test a second time?

These are all questions that you need to give some thought as you set out into the wonderful world of…

SLAYING THE ACT

ABOUT THE AUTHOR

Tina Wiles has a unique background. Not only does she hold a Bachelor's of Science degree in Industrial Engineering from the University of Michigan, but she is also a certified high school math teacher! Tina has been working in the test prep industry for over 13 years and has found her passion. She has published an ACT Workbook that she uses with all her students, and now she is teaching people across the world *How to Slay the ACT*. To gain more knowledge about the test and to understand what her students are going through, Tina takes the ACT herself 2-3 times a year. She resides in Naperville, IL with her amazing husband and their four sons.

Made in the USA
Lexington, KY
24 July 2019